The Present Preacher

The Present Preacher

Liz Shercliff
and
Matt Allen

© Liz Shercliff and Matt Allen 2021

First published in 2021 by the Canterbury Press Norwich
Editorial office
3rd Floor, Invicta House
108–114 Golden Lane
London EC1Y 0TG, UK
www.canterburypress.co.uk

Canterbury Press is an imprint of Hymns Ancient & Modern Ltd
(a registered charity)

Hymns Ancient & Modern® is a registered trademark of
Hymns Ancient & Modern Ltd
13A Hellesdon Park Road, Norwich,
Norfolk NR6 5DR, UK

All rights reserved. No part of this publication may be reproduced,
stored in a retrieval system, or transmitted,
in any form or by any means, electronic, mechanical,
photocopying or otherwise, without the prior permission of
the publisher, Canterbury Press.

The Authors have asserted their right under the Copyright, Designs and
Patents Act 1988 to be identified as the Authors of this Work

Acknowledgement is made for using quotations under copyright from:
The final verse and refrain of 'One more step along the world I go' (Sydney
Carter, 1915–2004) © 1971 Stainer & Bell Ltd, 23 Gruneisen Road, London
N3 1LS, www.stainer.co.uk, are used by permission. All rights reserved.
Tom Wright, Virtue Reborn is copyright © Nicholas Thomas Wright 2010.
Reproduced with permission of The Licensor through PLSclear.

Unless otherwise indicated, Scripture quotations are from the New Revised
Standard Version Bible: Anglicized Edition, copyright © 1989, 1995
National Council of the Churches of Christ in the United States of America.
Used by permission. All rights reserved worldwide.

British Library Cataloguing in Publication data

A catalogue record for this book is available
from the British Library

978-1-78622-386-9

Typeset by Regent Typesetting
Printed and bound in Great Britain by
CPI Group (UK) Ltd

Contents

Foreword by Deirdre Brower Latz	vii
Introduction	xi
1 Getting to the Present Matt Allen	1
2 Present to God Liz Shercliff	33
3 Present to Ourselves Liz Shercliff and Matt Allen	60
4 Present to the Bible Liz Shercliff and Matt Allen	87
5 Present to Our Congregations Liz Shercliff and Matt Allen	113
6 Present Preaching Various	144
Afterword by the Rt Revd Philip North	174
Bibliography	177
Index of Bible References	183
Index of Names and Subjects	185

Foreword

DEIRDRE BROWER LATZ

I am not sure how many sermons I've heard, or preached. If I had to guess, the cumulative total would be in the thousands. Among the sermons I've heard, I can honestly say that from time to time they spoke God to me – moved, compelled, wove into me, touched me, beckoned me from one place to another, and from those moments a ripple of transformation spread. Through a sermon I heard and received a call to preach. But, on reflection, it wasn't just the sermon, powerful though it was, it was also the preacher who dared to wrestle in public with scripture, who had learned to speak truth, and in so doing became an agent of God's speaking grace. My reflection raises all kinds of questions though, doesn't it? Who are we to preach? What kind of people dare to spring from an encounter with God into a courageous place speaking God? Who are we to be, we preachers?

Then, there is this: week after week, all over the world, eager-eared Christians still step (either physically or by a join button) into a space where their ordinary daily faith, the congregational life they participate in, and their hope in God-as-Alive-in-me are renewed: partly because of an encounter with God through a preacher's sermon. How are these sermons – and those who are preaching them – able to connect so powerfully, or subtly, so deeply, provocatively, prophetically or hopefully, with the kind of diverse hearts, unique lives and different people found in congregations all over the world?

This book, written by two preachers and teachers of preaching, is an eye-opening discussion that explores, discerns and challenges ideas of preaching, the preacher and the life of faith.

The possibility of transformation and genuine encounter with God, revealed in Christ, through the word, is one of the reasons Christians subject themselves to sermons. But, what kind of sermon, what kind of preaching, and what kind of preacher? Liz and Matt explore the possibilities of being the kind of preachers who are saturated in God's life, and who are abiding in God and God in them. Only then, from this place, laden with a willingness to discern, speak truth, wrestle openly, do they preach from a healthy centre and create sermons that enable the hearers to know that they are being re-created by God. I'm not doing justice to chapter after chapter that invite us in to a conversation with God, ourselves and the present preacher – plunge in and see!

Readable, this is not a *simple* book. It is loaded with a range of everyday examples and wide sources – from Fleabag to the poetry of Rabindranath Tagore (exactly!), Vicar of Dibley to creation scenes, but it is inescapably asking preachers to think deeply again about how our sermons are shaped around whole-heartedness for the present. The various chapters are unapologetically written in two clear voices – Liz and Matt offer reflections separately and have taken care to be themselves. This is a great gift – no pseudo 'we' and no merging of identities, instead we have a rich tapestry of theological framing which is unafraid to bring Barth and Ricœur into the room, alongside personable stories of encounters that reveal Godself in new ways to the authors when they are open to wrestling with scripture. There is an emphasis on honest clarity and each author cracks open their own life to share some of their learning with us. Sometimes this is a learning through darkness, suffering, and there is a sense throughout that each one is willing to be real.

When Liz and Matt's voices do join, they do so in harmony. They together place an emphasis on preaching as present practice, as theory honed by expectation that God does speak, and as complex, influenced by context, geo-political realities, and socio-economic worlds, as well as the character of the preacher and the listener. Their emphasis on 'now' and being the authentic self, on an honest acknowledgement of complex interpretations, and diversity of traditions, lets preachers from different worlds and church traditions explore preaching in new ways. This isn't a 'how to' manual of preaching, nor does it engage with whether or not preaching is still important (that is assumed) it's rather a 'join me in exploring' conversation that invites us to reflect deeply on who we are, as well as what, how, where and why we preach. It invites us into a space of honest contemplation about our preaching and our lives.

As a teacher of preaching – and as a preacher – I enjoyed the way this book invites the reader to stop. Pause. Think. Engage. Mull. I found that the questions unlocked ideas and thoughts that thickened my understanding of preaching. I heard my own history and echoes of formational preachers of the past came and went from the pages, honoured but also challenged, their voices amplified but not reified. Both Liz and Matt are seasoned preachers and reflective practitioners and it shows. There's an immense courage at work here – the vulnerability to describe the moments of enlightenment, or chastisement, reflection or critique make it into the book – and help us see that the brave-heart that is a whole-heart offers something rich to the preaching world. This book offers us something to chew on, at points it provokes, and – I think – it will drive us all back to Scripture to ask what new truths will emerge as we read with fresh eyes and hear with open ears. I felt the question lingered long after I finished reading: are you willing to have your own preaching practice challenged, reshaped, tweaked or reformed? Are you willing to encounter God newly so that your life is a preaching life?

As you plunge into this book and carve out the time to stop and ponder each chapter, I am sure that you too will encounter something of God who delights in creating us newly. The book points us towards the preaching life from a place of wholeness of heart that will stand us in good stead as preachers. As faith communities gather again to be shaped around the word and table, and as we wrestle together with what it means to be hope-bearing, authentic, resurgent people of peace, grief, lament and resurrection, we long to hear God speak. Thankfully, God speaks in many ways, including through faithful preachers of the word present in their wholeness, agents of grace in the world. As you step into the pages of this book, I hope that you will open your ears and heart, to receive God's shaping word.

Dr Deirdre Brower Latz
Principal and Senior Lecturer in Pastoral and Social Theology,
Nazarene Theological College, University of Manchester,
April 2021

Introduction

Many diligent and gifted preachers have shared faithfully, spoken passionately and, by the grace of God, seen transformation occur through God's Word in all kinds of churches. As you are reading this book, there is a good chance that you might be one of them. This book is not intended to offer you a shiny new approach to constructing a sermon, although it does contain some pointers. This book is not about biblical studies, but it will involve studying the Bible. This book is not about showing how preaching relates to apologetics, but it will draw some links between them. This book is not about any of those things because it is about you. It is a book about being a preacher for preachers. You are the present preacher and so are we. This book is about us, because our preaching is not: we are in it to point to Jesus.

The Present Preacher is about where we are now, who we are now, and what we need now to preach with passion, integrity and purpose. In short, we need to be prepared to be present. Present preachers know that the old and the new come together in the now.

Present preachers can own what they say and say what they own. Present preachers see the potential for preaching in life and the potential for life in preaching. Present preaching is not about information, but inspiration; not about posturing, but pastoring; not about credit, but credibility – it is where we speak personally about Jesus.

Throughout this book, we will speak personally. Sometimes as individuals and sometimes together. We begin by introducing ourselves and we invite you to do the same. In Chapter 1, we explore some homiletical theory and unpack the scriptural basis for our proposal. In the chapters which follow we explore all of the participants in preaching: God, ourselves, the scriptures and our congregations. Being present to all of these is the basis of what are calling the 'Now Homiletic'. That is, preaching that speaks in the present.

Liz

Introductions relate to the topic of the conversation, I think. At the start of a book on preaching it does not help you to know that I am a Mancunian, a United supporter, or a fan of live theatre. It might be relevant to know that I am a practical theologian, a member of the Editorial Board of *The Preacher* magazine, and that I have written on preaching before. But what seems really important is my relationship to preaching itself.

I love preaching! I love preaching whether I am doing it or am hearing it – as long as it is done well. In conversational matches about preaching's demise, I play defence; in debates about why Christians seem to know so little, I play striker. I believe in preaching as one of God's ways of nurturing, challenging and developing the people of God.

I do not believe in preaching as activity, but as a way of life. I do not believe in preaching that presumes that God will bless it when we have not given of our best. I believe in preaching as a gift, entrusted by God. I believe in preaching as words that we are to work carefully with full attention that we might craft something beautiful for God and the church.

I am used to preaching as contested space. I have been told that someone didn't listen because I am a woman. I have been told that my sermon was good so, because I am a woman, I must have got it from someone else. The sermon is contested space in a wider sense than that, though. History, theology, commentary, opinion, pastoral care, desire for popularity, the need to show off my intellect, all of these can, and do, fight for a slot in my sermons. But I am not preaching in the past, I am not preaching beyond the bounds of this congregation, I am not merely passing on informed opinion. I have been chosen, as today's preacher, to partner with God for the good of the People.

INTRODUCTION

I believe in now preaching – preaching that happens now, between speaker and hearers, that is for today.

But – as we will say later in this book – we need to know who we are when we come to preach, or indeed to read/write a book about preaching. 'We have this treasure in clay jars' (2 Corinthians 4.7), but what shape is the jar, and how does it give shape to what is inside?

This is who I am when I come to preach.

I am white, therefore privileged. I recognize in myself, and to my shame, the need to face up to the unearned privileges I have because of my skin colour.

I am a woman, therefore my 'voice' carries less weight than that of a man. I am part of a human group that is routinely silenced, oppressed and exploited.[1] When I read the Bible I am unlikely to read words a woman actually said (roughly 1.2% of the words in the Bible, including the Apocrypha, are spoken by women).[2]

I am educated. Currently I am studying for a Professional Doctorate in Practical Theology. This gives me access to a world not open to all, and confidence to interrogate it.

I don't have to worry about where my next meal is coming from (beyond the domestic discussion of who is cooking!).

I live in a village on the outskirts of Manchester, so have easy access to most things.

I have been seriously ill myself, and know what it is to live with anxiety.

Close members of my family have been suddenly struck down with life-threatening illness.

My parents divorced when I was young, and I was raised in an all-female household.

I have a younger sister.

I have a husband, a son, a daughter, three grandsons and a granddaughter.

I have been an evangelical, and I have not always believed in women's ordination.

Professionally I have usually been successful.

How does any of that affect the way I read the Bible, or impact on my preaching? Here's an example:

> The scribes and the Pharisees brought a woman who had been caught in adultery; making her stand before all of them, they said to him, 'Teacher, this woman was caught in the very act of committing adultery. Now in the law Moses commanded us to stone such women. Now what do you say?' They said this to test him, so that they might have some charge to bring against him. Jesus bent down and wrote with his finger on the ground. When they kept on questioning him, he straightened up and said to them, 'Let anyone among you who is without sin be the first to throw a stone at her.' And once again he bent down and wrote on the ground. When they heard it, they went away, one by one, beginning with the elders; and Jesus was left alone with the woman standing before him. Jesus straightened up and said to her, 'Woman, where are they? Has no one condemned you?' She said, 'No one, sir.' And Jesus said, 'Neither do I condemn you. Go your way, and from now on do not sin again.' *(John 8.3–11)*

The woman is brought by the powerful group. How often do I remain silent in the face of comments about people 'coming here for a better life' rather than point out that it is my own nation that produces the bombs destroying these people's homes?

The accusation they bring condemns her. How is she portrayed? Peter Sutcliffe, the Yorkshire Ripper, killed at least ten women. They were divided into two groups – prostitutes and innocent girls.[3] A senior West Yorkshire police officer, Jim Hobson, said in a 1979 press conference 'He has made it clear that he hates prostitutes ... Many people do ... but the Ripper is now killing innocent girls.' This woman is presented to Jesus with the easy assumption that he too will find her guilty. I haven't even got to the obvious fact that the powerful male group has protected one of its own by not also bringing the person the woman must have been found with!

The woman is not invited to speak, there is no defence,

the law is presented, and the question is whether or not Jesus would stone the woman. In the law of Moses, referred to by Pharisees, both adulterers were to be put to death but had to be caught in the act (Leviticus 20.10) but the Talmudic law changed so that circumstantial evidence was sufficient.[4] Too many preachers begin their reading of the passage by seeking to answer the Pharisees' question, would Jesus have stoned the woman had the case against her been proved? In doing so, they miss the essence of Jesus' dealings with both groups.

As an academic, I then want to ask where this story fits into John's account of the gospel. It is a later addition, and according to Elisabeth Schussler Fiorenza it places the woman at a crucial point in the development of John's text, indicating the pre-eminence of women in the Johannine community – so it isn't about a sinful woman, but about a woman being there when Jesus' ministry and mission take a specific turn.[5] Other questions come into play – was this adultery, or was the woman being exploited because she needed food? What was it like to be close to death at the hands of a mob? What effect has the usual telling of the story had on women in the Church?

It's not my intention to continue a discussion of this passage now – you will be able to develop your own ideas. At the end of this introduction there are some questions to help you write a similar introduction to yourself, but for now, meet Matt.

Matt

I have enjoyed working with Liz over a number of years. We have much in common, especially our love of preaching and our preference for theology that begins in practice rather than theory. However, I especially enjoy our collaborations because of our differences. In many ways we are quite unalike. Female and male, northerner and southerner, liberal and evangelical, Manchester United and Liverpool, and with a generational gap between us.

I come from a charismatic evangelical background, but these days I feel most at home within worship which has a distinctly

Anglican flavour. I have not lost my love for the Bible or my respect for God's authority expressed through it. However, I love being in a broad church like the Church of England. Here, I am encouraged by liberal voices who call me to honour lived experience and strive for social justice. Here, I am inspired by catholic voices who offer me treasures from Church history while ever holding out the manna and mystery of the Eucharist.

I currently work in theological education and training. Before that I was a parish priest. I have worked in Anglican churches and ecumenical partnerships. Aside from a brief stint as a student of mathematics, I have been in full-time church ministry my whole adult life. This means that my life has been both sheltered and exposed at the same time. Above all, I have learned that I cannot speak to others' experience. I can only live my story with God and seek to do so alongside others.

I was born into a Christian family and was raised going to church near where we lived. My parents worked hard at sharing their love of Jesus and impressing upon myself and my sister the value of being part of a Christian fellowship. I grew in faith in stages; I owned it for myself through an experience of God at a Soul Survivor Festival as a teenager and faced challenges that led to a renewal of commitment as a university student. At almost every stage in my journey, God has seemed to speak most powerfully to me through the ministry of leaders who are women. Women are in the majority in my top ten preacher list!

As I tell my story, I am conscious of my privilege as a white man. At times, I have felt a sense of entitlement about things many people simply would not dare to take for granted. However, I didn't grow up in a family where it was assumed I would go to university or pursue a professional career. My parents made significant sacrifices to support me in my choices. Many of my extended family are from working class backgrounds. Among their number are some very creative and entrepreneurial people, but almost all are not university educated. They have never considered that to be a necessary part of their journey. A good many of them have the happy knack of being able to speak directly, putting complex things in simple terms. They have modelled for me ways of knowing which seemed a

INTRODUCTION

world away from the theological study I embraced when my path led me to train for ordained ministry in my mid-twenties. When I first studied theology, I found it to be stuffy, self-satisfied and self-righteous, but also surprisingly safe. Once I acclimatized, I discovered I could play the game by using theology to prove learning and demonstrate that I belonged. Theology offered ways to make everything complex. It became something behind which I could hide, but not for long. The parish ministry and church leadership that followed my initial training demanded more of me than idle speculation about God.

I am a husband and a father. Both those roles mean a lot to me. My two children are in the early years of primary school and my family and I live in a village in Lancashire. I am unashamedly proud of my son and daughter, who are both fun, imaginative, witty and passionate people. Every day I am humbled by the persistent brilliance of my wife. She juggles more than I can imagine and is slowly teaching me how to be a better person.

In recent years, I have begun to integrate different chapters of my life and work out again what I have to say about my faith. This is what I have concluded: God may be an objective reality, but I do not think it is possible to know this without personal commitment.[6] In other words, I am not objective about the things of God or the person of Jesus. I should be concerned whenever I find myself pretending to be so. Liz offered a brief example of how her perspective informs her reading of scripture. Building on her example, I want to name something that I do when reading a Bible passage like the one she chose. In the past it seemed so obvious to me that it went unsaid, but it is important to who I am now that I own this: I trust the Bible's witness about Jesus; every time I read the Bible, above all, I look for Jesus and I look to Jesus.

Finally, I am a preacher and a teacher of preaching. Preaching is one of the most life-giving, time-consuming and nerve-jangling things that I do. I have high expectations of preachers. I am therefore keen to keep challenging myself to grow and inspiring others to do so too. I like the metaphor of a 'preaching toolbox' into which material and methods might be gathered to equip preachers to formulate their own style of preaching.[7] I find it useful to pick up homiletics books to hear someone else's enthusiasm for preaching and to encounter new ideas. As I have studied homiletics during my doctorate, I have become more aware of what it is I actually do as a preacher (which I share in Chapters 1 and 3). My hope is that this book helps you to do the same.

Other contributors

We are grateful to a number of friends and colleagues who have contributed to this book in different ways. You will meet them along the journey. They are Steve Murphy, Saju Muthalaly, Grace Thomas, Rich Wyld, Jenny Bridgman, Joel Love, Simon Moore, Tim Watson and Kate Bruce. Our special thanks go to Deirdre Brower Latz and +Philip North for writing the foreword and afterword.

Introduce yourself

Introducing ourselves in a linear fashion, as we have done above, risks making our identities sound static and hierarchical – as though the list might be ordered from most important to least. That of course, is not the case, and were we to write a second book in a year or two's time, I guess things would have changed and we would order things differently. So, in thinking about who you are, we would like you to use this method Liz used in some recent research.

Draw out four concentric circles, as the below figure. Beginning with the outer circle, jot down as many things about yourself as you can think of. As you work toward the centre, distil from the previous circle what you think are your most significant characteristics or experiences. In the centre you should be left with just a few words or phrases that represent the essence of who you think you are right now, in the present.

INTRODUCTION

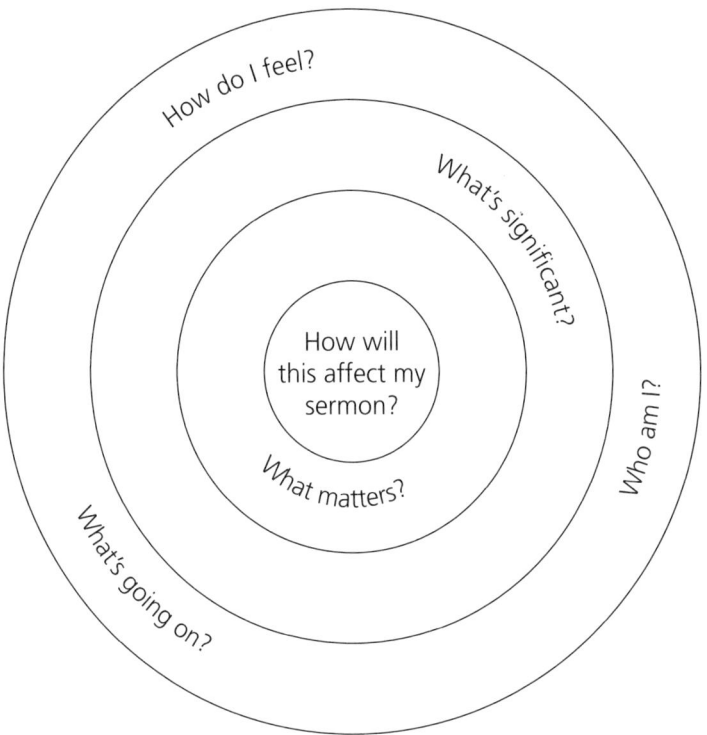

Notes

1 Elaine Storkey, 2015, *Scars Across Humanity: Understanding and Overcoming Violence Against Women*, London: SPCK. A great introduction to the ways in which this happens around the world.

2 L. Hardin Freeman, 2014, *Bible Women: All their Words and Why they Matter*, Kindle Edition, Forward Movement.

3 J. Smith, 2020, 'Covering Peter Sutcliffe's crimes, I saw that women weren't listened to – and they still aren't', *The Guardian*, 13 November, accessed 4.3.21.

4 D. Werner Amram, 'Adultery', from the *Jewish Encyclopedia*, https://jewishencyclopedia.com/articles/865-adultery, accessed 4.3.21.

5 Elisabeth Schussler Fiorenza, 1983, *In Memory of Her: A Feminist Theological Reconstruction of Christian Origins*, New York: Crossroad, p. 326.

6 Lesslie Newbigin discusses the idea of believing in order that we might know, which is found in the thinking of Augustine. This is con-

sistent with the way that obedience and faith unite in the scriptures. Practice and theory are not separated. L. Newbigin, 1995, *Proper Confidence: Faith, Doubt, and Certainty in Christian Discipleship*, London: SPCK, pp. 9–14.

7 K. Bruce, 2015, *Igniting the Heart: Preaching and Imagination*, London: SCM Press, p. 161.

I

Getting to the Present

MATT ALLEN

Why homiletics?

Preachers can exercise faithful ministries for decades without ever having to encounter the language of homiletics. They can become skilled and wise practitioners through their careful reading of scripture, observance of good examples, empathy with others, and openness to the Holy Spirit. So, we might ask: 'Who needs another book on preaching?' or even 'Why should we be interested in homiletics?' In short, I believe that developments in the area of homiletics over recent decades have been shaping preaching in churches. Some of these latest advances have put us in danger of forgetting things which are important about being a preacher.

So, what is homiletics? Well, if you think of preaching as playing the beautiful game (insert your preferred sport here), then homiletics is appreciation of the sport. It includes tactical analysis and punditry, commentary, facts and opinion as well as all that might support the development of the game itself. We are considering homiletics because this book is about being a preacher. As you read, please keep in mind the proper order of things. Preaching as part of Christian worship is directed towards far more than itself. Preaching does not happen to shape fresh thinking about homiletics but, importantly, fresh thinking about homiletics does happen to shape preaching.

Getting to the present

I like telling stories, although I am becoming more aware that when I do, I reveal more about myself than I probably intend. In this chapter we take a look at how we got to where we are today and why, for a time such as this, we need the present preacher. Right at the start, I want to acknowledge two things so that we can proceed with clarity and honesty as we explore the shifts that have happened in preaching within English-speaking Protestant churches. First, there are limits to what can be covered. This chapter will only focus on some of the key strands of the broad and diverse homiletical movement which became known as the New Homiletic. Secondly, I will inevitably tell this story in a way that mirrors my own journey of preaching – a trip I have taken on a seat with a restricted view.

I encountered the New Homiletic as something that felt truly 'new'. At the time, I didn't know there was a movement, let alone what it was called. I simply experienced the sermons of preachers who seemed to be doing something different from what I had known before. Hearing these preachers sparked my imagination and offered an example that helped me to develop as a preacher. Later, when I realized that they had been influenced by the New Homiletic, I discovered that I had found a place to call home within the world of preaching. Had the New Homiletic seemed less novel to me, this chapter would read differently. For those better acquainted with the preaching practised in Black American churches in the twentieth century, the New Homiletic and the preaching it encouraged was not all that new.[1] White Protestants came late to the party. Although most of the key figures behind the movement are white Protestant men, their enthusiasm and innovation within the New Homiletic ought not to be mistaken for invention.[2] It is all too easy for the New Homiletic to be feted for its impact on the discipline of homiletics in the academy. However, I try to remember that this highlights that some voices have had too little representation.

In this chapter, I will explore some of the developments in homiletics that have brought us to the present day. My main focus will be on the contribution of Karl Barth, the origins and emphases of the New Homiletic movement in the 1970s, and the trends in preaching which have emerged since. This chapter might be the one you skim read, skirt round, or soak up. It is deliberately focussed on theory and designed to help us to locate where we are in the present as preachers. Ultimately, I am arguing that the New Homiletic has done good things for preaching. However, in my view, it has been misleading for preachers because it discouraged them from preaching as themselves so that their personal faith was made evident.[3] It is time to reimagine the New Homiletic for present preaching. It is time for what we are calling the Now Homiletic.

> The Now Homiletic is about preachers
> being present,
> in the present,
> speaking personally,
> in Christ.

Throughout this book we are teasing out what the Now Homiletic means for us. I want us to begin our exploration in scripture.

Speaking personally

There's something about the tone of Paul's Second Letter to the Corinthians which I find compelling. It is rich in humility and seems so deeply and unashamedly personal. In this letter, Paul's emotions are evident. They bubble at the surface until the conflict inside him spills out quite dramatically in chapters 10 and 11.[4] In chapter 11, Paul reveals that love for the Corinthian church has been the motivation for the way he ministered among them.[5] It is this love which keeps Paul from making his letter *about* himself, yet he does speak *as* himself. Throughout the letter Paul models the balance of speaking personally without boasting – that is drawing attention to yourself and making things about you. Paul will boast only of his weakness.[6]

His letter is not an essay full of abstract ideas; it is a relatable and personal letter from an ordinary and extraordinary servant of Christ.[7] The verses which capture this best for me are a favourite of many.

> For we do not proclaim ourselves; we proclaim Jesus Christ as Lord and ourselves as your slaves for Jesus' sake. For it is the God who said, 'Let light shine out of darkness,' who has shone in our hearts to give the light of the knowledge of the glory of God in the face of Jesus Christ. But we have this treasure in clay jars, so that it may be made clear that this extraordinary power belongs to God and does not come from us. (2 Corinthians 4.5–7)

Looking around my kitchen at home, I can see lots of jars: jars of nuts, raisins, rice and seeds. All the jars are made of glass. This is a deliberate choice as it means your eye is drawn towards what is in them rather than the jar themselves. When I think about preaching, it is tempting to imagine myself as a glass jar. Surely this would be the best way to highlight the contents of the container? It certainly sounds like a virtue to be transparent. Being transparent is definitely positive if it means that you are visible and easy to spot. However, being transparent might also imply that someone can see through you. This works well in practice for the jars in my kitchen, but it does not sound like an unequivocally good thing when it comes to preaching. Let's identify the issue.

Even if glass jars like these had been an option, I want to argue that Paul would not have chosen them over the earthen vessels or 'clay jars'. The image Paul opts for is drawn from the Hebrew scriptures. It points to the ordinary dignity of human creatureliness and createdness; it acknowledges God as the potter and us as the clay.[8] The problem with a glass jar is that it has the potential to be illusory. A glass jar can almost suggest that it is not really there, that it is not altering the view of its contents. Yet, in reality, because of the thickness or curvature of the glass it will always be affecting what is seen, even if it is ever so slightly. A clay jar is apparent, it can be seen for what it is. Paul offers a picture of patently ordinary people as vessels of God's extraordinary power. A light has 'shone in our hearts' which is the 'light of the knowledge of the glory of God in the face of Jesus Christ'. This light is made visible to others as we bring out what God has done within us. This is personal. We are not seeing the treasure through the jar. We see the jar for what it is yet discover therein the treasure.

The wider argument of the letter helps us to explore further what it means to be a human vessel of divine power. In 2 Corinthians 5.16, Paul writes about no longer regarding anyone 'according to the flesh' or 'from a human point of view'.[9] For Paul, 'the flesh' represents hostility and opposition towards God, especially God's Spirit.[10] I think Paul is suggesting that we set aside the standards and criteria by which we are often inclined to judge other human beings. Instead, we should choose to be open and receptive to what God might be revealing through them. This makes sense of what Paul goes on to say in reference to Jesus as he writes:

> though we once knew Christ from a human point of view, we know him no longer in that way. So if anyone is in Christ, there is a new creation: everything old has passed away; see, everything has become new! (2 Corinthians 5.16b–17)

The new creation Paul discovers in Christ enables him to differentiate between two types of knowing.[11] Paul initially *only* knew Jesus as a person from a specific cultural background located in time and space.[12] This as a way of knowing was limited by solely using human categories: knowing 'according to the flesh'. When we label and classify people in this way, it is limiting and resistant to what might be revealed of God in them. Having come to see what has been revealed and realized of God in Christ, Paul now knows Jesus in a different way which is not 'according to the flesh'. Paul's openness to the work of God is transformed. This new creation which is found in Christ can be seen also in others who, by faith, have union with Christ.[13]

Now at this point we need to be clear. Some theologians have overstretched the point of what knowing 'according to flesh' means and have downplayed the importance of investigating and seeking to understand the Jesus of history.[14] This would be to ignore the voice of scripture as a whole and wander towards a form of docetism. The extraordinary thing is that it is through the historical Jesus, the Word made flesh of John's Gospel, that Paul and we discover most fully that God dwells in and speaks through human beings – divine power *in* human corruptibility and weakness.[15] It is both the hope and mystery of those who belong to Jesus that his Spirit dwells within them.[16] Put another way, we encounter others 'through the flesh' but we must be willing to know them by more than our 'fleshly' categories to discover the treasure in those clay jars.

Above all, in 2 Corinthians, faith in Christ (and therefore union with Christ) is the key and decisive factor in our identity. It is the basis on which we speak. In 2 Corinthians 2.17, Paul writes 'For we are not peddlers of God's word like so many; but in Christ we speak as persons of sincerity, as persons sent from God and standing in his presence'. Sincerity stands out to me. The Greek word on which it is based only occurs a few times in the New Testament and it points towards purity of motive and frankness.[17] The preacher ought to be one who is, in Christ, a person of sincerity sent from God. Digging deeper into this verse, it seems to me to be about the core identity of the preacher. A more literal translation of the Greek text of the second part of the verse reveals its beauty, depth and poetry. It reads: 'but as of God before God in Christ we speak.'[18] This translation has become my 'vestry prayer' before I preach. I think it captures who we are as preachers.

but as of God, before God, in Christ we speak.

I believe that every human being is 'of God' and we all live our lives 'before God', whether we acknowledge that or not. Preachers are to acknowledge that they are of God and before God and speak specifically as those 'in Christ'. Being in Christ is a striking feature of Paul's letters worthy of far greater investigation than possible here. I think of it as a conscious way of perceiving everything differently 'in newness of life' having been buried with Jesus 'by baptism into death'.[19] I explore what this means to me a little more in Chapter 3.

Later in his letter, Paul adds that 'we are ambassadors for Christ, since God is making his appeal through us'.[20] An ambassador is one who represents someone else. They are present to re-present the one who sent them. There is no anonymous messenger, nor a disembodied message. There is a person who shows up to be encountered. As clay jar preachers, we are called to be ambassadors. We speak personally, passionately and sincerely out of who we are in Christ. As hearers of preaching, we receive those who speak as being in Christ themselves. We receive them as those prepared to be open to the work of God through them and the word of God to us.

Barth and the invisible glass jar

When I began training for ordained ministry, I met people quite different from those I grew up around. One new friend was a bookish chap who had a particular passion for understanding the Bible. He had a strong grasp of historical criticism and would happily argue that important theological insights are gained by understanding the background to biblical texts. It also seemed to me that he had an odd fascination with twentieth century theologians. At times, I was sure that he mentioned Karl Barth as least once in every conversation I had with him. As it turns out, my friend was onto something. What he had found in Barth was a primary impulse which resonated with his own story.

Barth had an unabated passion to redraw the lines of theology in the light of what God has revealed through his Word, that is Jesus. Jesus is God's directly revealed Word, scripture is the primary witness to God's revelation, and proclamation in the community of faith is a secondary witness.[21] Theology is unable to access and interpret God's Word itself, it only interprets in relation to the Word's witnesses.[22] What had lifted my friend's head out of books and brought him to train for

Christian ministry was his life-changing encounter with the living God, the same God who showed up as an actual person in human history. Reading Barth helped my friend to keep theology in its place by reminding him that he was a student of the Bible because he was a follower of Jesus – surely that is always a game-changer.

If you have read the introduction to this book, you will have already spotted why I like Barth. I appreciate the way he is often unashamedly unambiguous. He regularly deals in sharp lines, clear distinctions and bold colours. I was once asked to write an essay on whether the faith (or lack of faith) of interpreters should make a difference to their interpretation of biblical texts – Barth says yes! He outright rejected the idea that human methods of biblical interpretation can take hold of the revelation of God.[23] The meaning of scripture is not something that can be objectively determined through historic inquiry.[24] Barth is unwilling to say that scripture simply *is* revelation.[25] Instead, the Bible *becomes* the Word of God when it is recognized for what it is and read and heard with faith.[26] I like where Barth is coming from, but when he talks about preaching there is a snag: Barth seems to want invisible glass jar preachers. Let's consider why.

I am a still a big fan of BBC's classic comedy *The Vicar of Dibley* which seems to have stood the test of time. One of my favourite scenes, reprised in a later episode, is when Geraldine walks along a lane with her boyfriend, playfully jumping in puddles. All is well until she jumps into what looks like a puddle but actually turns out to be a hole several feet deep and finds herself immersed up to her armpits in freezing cold water. When it comes to Barth's approach to theology and preaching,[27] on the road in front of us is what might look like a shallow puddle but is instead a deep hole. It has to do with Barth's rejection of the *analogia entis* or 'analogy of being'.[28] Barth argues that the relationship that exists between God and human beings is on the basis of the grace of God alone and not 'ontological correspondence' between them.[29] We cannot completely avoid this puddle, but we'll try not to be immersed in it.

There is a huge depth of feeling in Barth's writing, especially as he expresses his utter dismay at the German Christians who thought their faith compatible with Nazi ideology. Barth took aim at their version of natural theology – the idea that God's revelation can be apprehended through observation of nature or history.[30] For Barth, nature and grace cannot sit alongside one another; grace is a miracle that cannot be treated like any phenomenon of this world.[31] Centuries earlier, the Reformation in Europe had showed how to parachute out of a church which seemed stuck on auto pilot to destruction. In his own time, Barth jumped and pulled the cord. His writing grabbed hold of the Protestant doctrine of *sola gratia* and Martin Luther's *simul iustus et peccator*; it reasserted that human beings remain sinful and are only *considered* righteous through participation in Christ's righteousness.[32] Instead of the 'analogy of being', Barth describes the 'analogy of faith' which re-establishes a point of contact between God and human beings in Christ; it is only real in faith and never possessed by the believer.[33]

Barth had seen a stark example of what happens when people do 'what was right in their own eyes'.[34] Given his life experience, it is not hard to see why he wants invisible preachers who are sceptical of what they bring. As I mentioned earlier, glass jar preaching seems to have a lot going for it in theory. It is definitely worth bearing in mind as a corrective when we are in danger of being full of ourselves. I find it helpful how Barth clarifies how human words relate to the Word of God by offering these two simple formulas: Preaching is about what God speaks; and preaching is about the church's obligation to serve God's Word. The basic idea is that God employs the words used by preachers, who are duly called, as they exposit biblical texts in ways which are relevant in the community of faith, hinting towards what God may be saying.[35] The task of the preacher is to make sure that are following the 'movement of thought in the text', not a plan that comes from it.[36] At all times, God remains sovereign in revelation; biblical interpretation and preaching are both matters of faith which begin and end in God.[37]

Barth is a giant in the world of homiletics, offering more than we see at face value. He highlights the extraordinary potential of preaching. The seeds of what is possible are planted deep within his work. However, what we see on the surface can look odd. Famously, Barth discouraged preachers from using introductions or conclusions, and he gave short shrift to attempts at indicating relevance or suggesting application.[38] Preachers become invisible glass jars: they give sermons shape and form but are attempting not to be seen. As I think about my own background, hearing good expository preaching has been vital in my faith development. Yet as I hear Barth describe it, I am reminded how misleading it is when preachers try to 'purely' teach what the Bible says, or simply see their role as facelessly declaring the mighty acts of God. However, in this, there is more to Barth than meets the eye. While suspicious of anything of themselves that the preacher brings, crucially, at the same time, he advocates an approach that relies entirely on the preacher's 'proper attitude' – an expectation that God will speak.[39] Despite his nervousness about human sinfulness and natural theology, Barth is flicking the switch that would light up the world of homiletics. The sermon is a contemporary event of revelation; preachers ought to be people of faith; people who preach expecting God to always be speaking now.

Deductive preaching and the measuring jug

I wonder what you think of as 'typical preaching'. Before the New Homiletic arrived on the scene, one form in particular was predominant in Western Protestant churches – deductive preaching. In a potted history of preaching, a decisive shift occurred when the Church was influenced by the privileging of reason over imagination in Greco-Roman culture.[40] Rather than being about invitation, with reason taking the lead preaching became about persuasion and eventually primarily about explanation.[41] The Middle Ages brought the 'university sermon', where a main theme is divided into three parts which are each explained.[42] (The university sermon is not the same thing as sermons written for a university context which came later in church history.[43]) The Reformation saw the development of the Puritan 'plain' sermon. In keeping with its name, this style of preaching was intended to be clear and understandable to its listeners.[44] Sermons would typically begin with exegesis, move towards doctrine and instruction, then finish with what might be a lengthy portion of practical application.[45] Finally, a further form of preaching arose which would become the dominant form of preaching at the time the New Homiletic was birthed – 'three points and a poem'.[46] All of these types of sermon, while different, have this one thing in common: they are forms of preaching which use what is known as deductive movement.

The description of the different forms of deductive sermons may have been familiar to you. Maybe you have preached sermons like these. In deductive preaching, talks move from the general to the specific. They are developed around exegesis or explanation which is followed by application. Deductive sermons therefore tend to be propositional. The point is that the preacher makes their point, proves their point, and points the persuaded hearer forward. I have certainly heard some excellent sermons structured along similar lines. It is true that we encounter general principles in the scriptures, especially when they are read as a whole. Skilled preachers can employ creative techniques to illustrate the points they wish to make. In recent decades, the art of what has been called developmental sermons has been rearticulated, showing how sermons can be usefully and creatively developed around a key idea or claim from the text.[47] However, it is still the case that preaching which places reason over imagination and that seeks to explain rather than invite, might easily become tired and predictable and fail to connect with hearers.

As preachers of exclusively deductive sermons, there is a danger that we have this treasure in a measuring jug. The task of preaching involves overlaying a plan over the biblical text and identifying, codifying and presenting information. The preacher is only there to point to the general so we can measure off what we need to apply. The New Homiletic arrived on the scene with an alternative. The movement showed how preaching can be more than a message from the past, mean more than a theory to be applied, and do more now than we ever thought possible. The New Homiletic would seek to turn the logic of preaching on its head.

The New Hermeneutic and the now

A twentieth-century development in biblical interpretation known as the New Hermeneutic provided the foundations on which the New Homiletic built. Barth was a key influence behind the New Hermeneutic which focussed its attention on how God might be speaking *now* through the Bible.[48] In the twentieth century, the ability of language to construct reality, not just name it, was a hot topic of discussion in the academy.[49] At the same time, thought in the field of biblical hermeneutics was being reshaped. There was a pervading sense that the Bible was not being interpreted in ways that led to lives being transformed now.[50] There was a growing awareness of the importance of considering the 'horizons' of the author, text and reader.[51] The world of the author had been the subject of historical critical inquiry, but this world 'behind the text' was not the only world to be explored. The world in front of the text, belonging to the reader, and the world of the text itself each provided a further place of encounter with God in the now.[52] Barth had drawn attention to the 'movement of thought in the text' which shaped how texts communicated. Paul Ricœur focussed on the ability of the biblical text to create an inhabitable world for its reader.[53] Barth and Ricœur shared a common desire to discover the Word of God through the witness of the biblical texts.[54] Renewed attention was given to the fusion of the horizons of the text and the reader; the interest was in the effect of words rather than the concepts conveyed by them.[55] The New Hermeneutic made its point loud and clear: overemphasizing what texts *say* risks missing what texts *do*. The exciting rediscovery that biblical texts *do* something is the ground onto which the New Homiletic built and into which it planted its flag.

The New Homiletic

In 1971, around the same time Gene Wilder first donned a top hat to welcome guests to a fictional chocolate factory and Sean Connery ended his stint as James Bond (the first time) in *Diamonds are Forever*, Fred Craddock wrote a book worth heralding as 'ground zero' for an explosion of colour, energy and creativity in homiletics.[56] Craddock's book, *As One Without Authority*, lamented the failure of preaching to really connect with people. Words had lost their power, there were new questions about what was 'real', and preachers were waking up to discover that the relationship they might have thought they had with their hearers had changed overnight with the dawning of post-Christendom.[57] If preachers were licensed to thrill then they were working undercover. Listening to sermons, as it turned out, was not proving to be a golden ticket for hearers.

Thankfully, Craddock didn't write a book to lament the state of preaching but, instead, offered a 'theology of speaking' which acknowledged the extraordinary amount of interest being taken into communication, language and meaning.[58] Both David Randolph and Craddock had been influenced by the new hermeneutic and the idea that the language of the Bible does something as well as says something, generating events that can be experienced.[59] Randolph, who is commonly credited for coining the term 'New Homiletic', was interested in what sermons might do in the lives of their hearers; Craddock however led the way in presenting and promoting the eventfulness of preaching.[60] Craddock reimagined the preaching event shaped around theology, taking a radical approach to homiletics in the academy and to sermons in churches. Essentially, he asked and began to answer the key question at this pivotal time: 'Where is God in this?'

Craddock's theology of speaking made a massive contribution to homiletics. It challenged the almost unthinking assumption that understanding precedes words; sometimes words precede understanding.[61] This is true for the Word of God, which interprets us.[62] We engage with the scriptures so that we might be addressed by God in the present, discovering the Word of God in the movement, conversation and communication that happen between Church and scripture.[63] Craddock builds his theology based on Barth's position which asserted that God's revelation is current, live, and contemporary and that as listeners and readers we bring our questions and issues to the text hoping to encounter God's Word through the scriptures.[64] The New Homiletic developed the idea that if this is how we think God speaks, this should be shown by how we speak as preachers. As preachers, we haven't completed the work of biblical interpretation, the sermon itself is an event of interpretation; it is 'a happening' for its hearers.[65]

At this point, it is worth identifying all of the participants in preaching. They are the preacher, the hearers and the Bible. Often these are depicted as an equilateral triangle with labels at the three vertices. The Bible at the apex, the preacher on the left, and the congregation on the right. This is known, rather aptly, as the 'Preaching Triangle'.[66] God's activity is not limited or confined to the Bible, Preacher or Hearers. So, the question 'Where is God in this?' is answered by recognizing that God is all over this, everywhere. We will see how the New Homiletic attended to each of the participants and the interactions between them.

As with any movement, there were others who questioned the dominant paradigm in preaching before the 1970s and whose work influenced what was to come.[67] However, I will focus our attention on Craddock, giving honourable mention to David Buttrick and Eugene Lowry. Although the different participants in preaching cannot fully be separated, I explore Craddock's thinking by working round the preaching triangle in this order: Bible, Hearers, Preacher. After noting the emergence of the New Homiletic. I will share my thoughts on its legacy as we aim to get to the present.

Bible

The New Homiletic is about preaching the Bible more on its own terms. Craddock asked searching questions of preachers who stuck rigidly to deductive propositional preaching. Picture this preacher organizing the sermons they have preached on a wide range of biblical texts. The scriptures on which their talks were based represent a variety of forms of literature, but the sermon texts are uniform by comparison. If sermons are to do the same as the text is doing, they need to retain the form as well as the content of the biblical text in their design.[68] If preachers are always aiming to identify themes and make points, they run the risk of boiling off the water and preaching what Craddock called the stain which is left at the bottom of the mug.[69] It is not that the form of the biblical text must be imitated in sermons, but doing so can strengthen them; it is desirable that narrative is communicated through narrative sermons, parables are explored parabolically and so on.[70] The New Homiletic developed a particular preference for narrative sermons because in scripture, God's dealings with human beings are largely shaped by narrative.[71]

Hearers

The New Homiletic is concerned with how hearers experience the sermon and encounter God's Word in the preaching event. The question wasn't about how to form an argument but rather how language might be used so the sermon connects with hearers and stirs them into a response.[72] Changing the 'movement' of talks could mean that hearers can play a greater role in the preaching event. In deductive movement general or universal truth claims are identified, then given particular application.[73] Sermons shaped using inductive movement work in a different way. They express themselves more indicatively than imperatively; they attempt to *show* hearers how it is rather than *tell* hearers what to do. It is down to the hearer to work out what then will be.[74] The congregation then are no longer passive recipients of the preaching event but active participants in it.

The vital importance of language and imagination in preaching is underlined by the statement above in the idea that hearers can be *shown* something through the spoken word. The inductive method makes significant demands on the imagination of preachers; it is easier to reflect upon our experience than attempt to recreate it for others.[75] Preachers need figurative language which creates images, rather than literal language which shapes concepts.[76] The notion that sermons employ rhetorical devices is not new. What is new is how these figurative forms of language were seen in the New Homiletic.[77] Metaphoric language and stories are not optional ways of enhancing the points being made, they are not there to 'bring home' a message to hearers; they are there to create a space for hearers of the sermon.[78] Imagination has many functions for preachers.[79] It is most visible when it enables the expression of image-filled language, but it begins with the impression of images upon the preacher.[80]

The New Homiletic encourages preachers to be sensitive to what is happening around them.[81] This sensitivity extends to their awareness of their congregation. Preaching in the inductive method does not depend on an authority which comes from a certain amount of distance, it requires being present as part of the congregation yourself.[82] In this way, Craddock particularly emphasizes the empathic function of imagination. This is important at every stage of preparing a sermon. When preachers go on the 'white water rafting trip of biblical exegesis', Craddock insisted they should take their congregations 'along on the trip' instead of going it alone and bringing them back a keyring.[83] The preacher and the congregation are to share in the experience of engaging with and exploring the biblical text, rather than the preacher bringing the congregation some points that came out of their engagement with the text.[84]

Preacher

The New Homiletic emphasizes method over content.[85] How preachers preach is a large part of what they preach; the process is as important the outcome.[86] Furthermore, *how* you preach is theological: it gives others insight into what you believe; it may be more telling and honest than *what* you preach.[87] Craddock was not naïve about the ethics of adopting the approaches to preaching he proposed. Preachers need to be mindful of the extremes of certitude and confusion; they ought to make the method and content of their sermons 'a matter of conscience and conviction'.[88] However, consideration of the person of the preacher was underdeveloped in Craddock's initial thinking; he paid the preacher more attention in his later work to underline this key point: preaching is self-disclosive; it is the faith of preachers which gives them credibility.[89]

The legacy of the New Homiletic

With the benefit of hindsight, we can see that Craddock's work blazed a trail for others who would build on his work to create the New Homiletic movement. They would share a focus on the experience of hearers in the preaching event. They would think about the way language might be employed in imaginative and creative ways. They would help preachers to think about the form of their sermons in terms of what it was they were trying to do. Outstanding contributions were made by Buttrick and Lowry.

In his *Homiletic: Moves and Structures*, Buttrick proposed that instead of making points, preachers made movements of language which he called moves. These moves combined what he called 'theological smarts and rhetorical skill'.[90] Buttrick's structures include guidance on shaping of the plot of sermons in line with the preacher's intention.[91] Buttrick also identified three locations in consciousness which prompted different approaches to the design of sermons. He called these immediacy, reflection and praxis.[92] Immediacy invites hearers to immerse themselves in a story and find points of contact within their own experience which help them to identify a response.[93] Reflection involves finding themes and topics within passages which can be explored.[94] Praxis begins in the reality of people's lives, it addresses them directly first, rather than following a theme led from the scriptures.[95] What Buttrick did was to look at the phenomenon of preaching itself, identify what was happening, and suggest how preachers could rethink what they were doing in the light of what they wanted to be heard or experienced by the congregation. The emphasis was on the hearers of the sermon.

Lowry's work developed the idea of the plot of sermons differently. He was happy to locate his work within the New Homiletic and saw preaching as an event within an act of worship which intends and anticipates a meeting between God and people.[96] In an expanded edition of his original work, Lowry's main thesis is that sermons ought to be regarded 'as a homiletical plot, a narrative art form, a sacred story'.[97] The preacher is an artist and storyteller.[98] Lowry describes the shape of the homiletical plot in his 'Lowry loop', which outlines these five stages of a typical sermon depicted in the shape of a loop:

1. upsetting the equilibrium,
2. analysing the discrepancy,
3. disclosing the clue to resolution,
4. experiencing the gospel,
5. anticipating the consequences.[99]

Evident in these stages is a focus on the experience of hearers, specifically that the gospel is encountered as the key to bringing about a shift or change. It is easy to dismiss Lowry's work for being too formulaic, but to do so underestimates the utility of what he proposes. Similar schemes are still prominent in teaching new preachers how to shape sermons.[100] Lowry's contribution to the New Homiletic was to offer a clear approach to narrative preaching with a theological basis formed through the insights of the new hermeneutic.[101] This approach could be used for a range of texts so that they could be preached with a narrative shape. However, with the focus on the form of sermons, other things were neglected.

It is vital to remember that the New Homiletic was formed partly in response to culture change and the rejection of traditional and institutional authority. It encouraged sermons that invited hearers to share in the journey of discovery in the biblical stories, rather than offering them propositions and points extracted from the Bible by an authoritative preacher. A new relationship was developing between speakers and hearers as preachers contended with the loss of a supportive culture in the 1960s and 1970s.[102] The good news of Jesus was to be displayed on its own merits so that people might recognize its distinctive claims and weigh up their responses.[103] There is no doubt in my mind that the New Homiletic made an important and timely contribution to preaching. It reminded preachers that shaping sermons using inductive and narrative approaches can help them to be a place of encounter with God where hearers can experience the biblical text in all its dimensions through their imagination, emotions and reason.[104] But all of this came at a cost.

The New Homiletic and the metal teapot

Fifty years since its advent, the New Homiletic has inevitably faced critique. Some said that overemphasizing the form of sermons led to reduced theological content.[105] Others cautioned against over-reliance on narrative forms and expressed concern that the desire to create experiences in preaching had shifted authority away from the Bible to the hearers.[106] It is true that New Homiletic represented a shift in authority. However, it was intended to be a shift away from the authority of the preacher, rather than away from the biblical text. If we compare the deductive preaching dominant in white Protestant churches to the inductive preaching of the New Homiletic, their differences are stark. Instead of preachers journeying in the world behind the text so that they might tell hearers what the Bible says, preachers were now holding open the world of the text so that they might show hearers what the Bible does. The preacher had been an authority figure who could explain the text to the hearers. The preacher became a storyteller who facilitates the encounter between the text and the hearer. The New Homiletic encouraged preaching which sought to fuse the horizons of the hearers and the text. But this has led to preaching which downplayed the fusion of the horizons of the preacher and the text.

This is the problem with the New Homiletic. Somewhere along the way we forgot just how important it is to speak personally. We found a new way to demonstrate a mastery over the text which avoided our 'clayness'. Now we have this treasure in a metal teapot (or perhaps a disco ball). The preacher can be like a mirror, showing the hearers themselves while remaining hidden in plain sight. I think it is good to find ways to enable hearers to see themselves as part of the sermon. I like the idea of dazzling sermons, but if downplaying the preacher's authority has led to masking the preacher's authorship and ignoring their authenticity then something has gone wrong. Downplaying of the person of the preacher is the central flaw of the New Homiletic. Craddock had warned that *how* we preach is theological. Behind that 'how' is a 'who' and a 'why' which require fresh consideration to restore the preacher to sermons. We will explore these further in Chapter 3. At this point, it is useful to look at how other writers in the field of homiletics have sought to clarify both the identity and the aims of preachers and so pointed the way beyond the New Homiletic.

The present

Anyone who has heard me talk about homiletics for longer than five minutes will have heard me mention Thomas Long. Earlier, I referred to my friend who was a little obsessed with Karl Barth. Well, maybe I am not so different after all! In his *The Witness of Preaching*, Long offers an answer to the question 'Who is the preacher?' Preachers, he explains, have been depicted by the 'master images' of 'herald', 'storyteller/

poet' and 'pastor'.[107] The preacher as herald is focused on the content of their sermons, keen above anything else to be faithful to God's message in scripture as they have received it.[108] The preacher as pastor seeks to find creative ways to reach hearers and address their needs.[109] The preacher as storyteller/poet seeks a coming together of hearers' stories and God's story, just like in the New Homiletic.[110] However, there is an alternative image which draws together the strengths of these three master images: the preacher as a witness.[111] A witness is authoritative because of what they have seen and heard firsthand, rather than through status, power or rank.[112] Like Barth, Long emphasizes God's freedom in self-revelation: we may be preaching, but it is more important that we hear how Jesus is speaking.[113] I am convinced by Long's argument and the strong biblical basis he identifies for it, but in a few areas I want to press further than he seems prepared to go.

Ever since I was first allured by the gleam of the purple and gold school prefect badge and the power I imagined it could yield, I have been aware that my love of having a role is not always a good thing. There is a growing swell of voices seeing the potential for preaching to be a place for speaking personally about faith.[114] Liz and I are joining that chorus with our own distinctive tune. We want to sound a warning about roles. Roles are ways of concealing self and self-interest. In Chapter 3 we show how the role of preacher raises enough issues of its own. To be fair to Long, he is clear that being a witness doesn't imply neutrality; experience of God's truth is always partial and disinterested readings of scripture are impossible and unhelpful.[115] Witnesses need to be shown to be sincere. However, the role can still take over a little and mask the person. I think Long overstates the extent to which we can hear on behalf of others and understates the importance of reflexivity. It is good to share what we see and hear, but it is even better if we know why we see what we see and hear what we hear. Roles can hinder us from knowing when we are really speaking personally. The present preacher, as I will show below, is all about being present as yourself – present in the preparation and present in the now of preaching. I like the 'witness' badge as a preacher but I won't be pinning it on my chest because I think it might get in the way.

The New Homiletic was a response to culture change. As we move past the New Homiletic, it is worth asking what has changed since. The cold hard reality is that, outside of perhaps a committed core of seasoned Christians, biblical literacy is at a low ebb and preachers cannot assume that people have the tools to make connections between their stories and the stories of scripture.[116] Alyce McKenzie suggests that narrative preaching needs adapting for smaller screens and shorter attention spans.[117] Preachers should 'make a scene' in their preaching by breaking up larger stories into smaller segments.[118] Mixing up scenes means allowing for different forms of communication and content to co-exist.[119] I see similarities between McKenzie 'scenes' and Buttrick's 'moves'. Others have described this sort of approach as episodic preaching. I like the idea of sermons being made of scenes which can stand alone, while together offering a coherent story which, in turn, serves as a potential trailer for the feature length movie of God's story.[120] When I read homiletics books like McKenzie's, it is tempting to look for tips and ideas that inspire me to be more creative and innovative. There's nothing wrong with this. Present preaching ought to be both of those things. However, the real challenge hits at a personal level. Where the New Homiletic had a tendency towards facile plots, and simplistic answers, the preacher needs to offer more authenticity, not just greater creativity.[121]

Preachers are to be seekers of wisdom who attend to the presence of God in their own life, the text and in community life.[122] Drawing on Nancy Lammers Gross's work on the silencing of women's voices in preaching, McKenzie concludes that preachers must be able to speak freely, precisely and courageously about what they notice and experience.[123] Long talked about preachers witnessing to what they have seen and heard. McKenzie makes it clear that this should include what preachers have *noticed* and *experienced*, including through affectivity. In other words, we preach because what we have to share matters to us, it has affected us. This takes us within touching distance of what it means to be a present preacher.

GETTING TO THE PRESENT

The present preacher and the Now Homiletic

Many years later, I can still feel the goosebumps and recall my sharp intake of breath at the moment the priest stood at the table, raised her outstretched arms and prayed:

> Be present, be present,
> Lord Jesus Christ,
> our risen high priest;
> make yourself known in the breaking of bread.
> Amen.[124]

In that Easter act of worship, I experienced this prayer of preparation at the table, based on the Emmaus story in Luke 24, in a new and powerful way. It was then it struck me at a deeper level that in the Eucharist we expect and long for Jesus to be present and make himself known to us in the present. As Christians, general notions about disembodied experiences of God's presence are challenged by the reality and physicality of Christ's bodily resurrection.

The present preacher is the one who shows up and makes themselves known. Both in sermon preparation and as they speak, they are committed to being present. As a practical theologian, I am convinced that we express our theology through what we do, what we say, and what we say we are doing.[125] Preaching is theological, not applied theology.[126] How we preach shows what we believe. I think Barth was right that preachers should have a faith that expects God to be speaking now through the scriptures. It makes no sense that this should be concealed by preaching practices that hide the basis on which such preaching depends. We need the preacher to be present. When we put ourselves out there as a visible flesh and blood preacher, owning what we say, we offer our sermons as personal speech in the now, for the now, demonstrating faith that God will be speaking now. This is the heart of the Now Homiletic.

In the Now Homiletic, the inductive movement encouraged in the New Homiletic begins close to home in the person of the preacher. The preacher can be present as themselves, freed from any pretence towards objectivity or mastery. I am a practical theologian because I love theology which begins in the particular and the concrete, rather than the general and abstract.[127] Theology is always personal. This is not to say that there are not boundaries. Other Christian theologians will rightly point out that inductive approaches can downplay Christian tradition and lead to relativism.[128] However, I think that this is addressed by taking seriously what it means to be 'in Christ'. I am not saying that we find answers *in* ourselves but that we find answers *as* ourselves in Christ. In Christ we discover our true identity, the inheritance of faith, and the challenge of radical relationality. Because we are in Christ, as preachers we cannot abandon Christian tradition, but recognize that we can speak personally about that too.

Present preaching is partnered to apologetics because it is about speaking personally about what faith means to us. Apologetics is not about arguing the claims of Christianity on the basis of rationality but sharing Christian hope on the grounds of faith. It is less about me trying to convince others about the good news of Jesus, and more about sharing with them why I am convinced. It certainly ends theologically but it begins autobiographically.[129] As preachers, we can honestly witness to the faith we have, not the faith we aspire to. God's revelation is not within our gift and God's power does not despise fragile ordinary vessels.

It took a global pandemic, when it had never been easier to participate in the worship of other church communities, to remind me of the value of being addressed by those I know personally. As it turned out, we didn't need people who can write sermons as much as we needed preachers who would find ways to be present. Things we might have assumed to be permanent about the context for preaching had been shifted and shelved in response to coronavirus. It was therefore all the more important, in such a time, that as preachers we were willing to be present to all of the task of preaching. This means knowing who we are and why we preach. We want to be preachers who come as we are in Christ to be present to God, present to ourselves, present to the Bible and present to our congregations. We do not need to hide or pretend; we know we have this treasure in clay jars.

Paul's Second Letter to the Corinthians offers the foundations for what we propose in this book. It has helped me to clarify what I think is important for preaching in the present. It is those who have an authentic faith who are sent by God to preach. It is because we believe and identify ourselves as being in Christ that we speak.[130] We have been affected by what we are sharing, we haven't got to pretend that we aren't there, and it's okay to be clay. As present preachers, we are earthen vessels to be seen for who we are without artifice or illusion. Being a preacher is not about drawing attention to ourselves but showing up and speaking personally so that the treasure within us might be clearly distinguished as the work and power of God.

As of God, before God, in Christ we speak.

Questions for further reflection

- What does it mean to you to speak personally as a preacher?
- Have you ever listened to a preacher and thought about how their approach to preaching was an expression of their faith? What did you notice?
- Have we so focussed on what we are doing in preaching that we have forgotten what it is to *be* a preacher?
- Which of the containers mentioned in this chapter best describes you as a preacher? Glass jar? Clay jar? Measuring jug? Metal teapot? Something else?
- In what ways might you be more present in your preaching?

Notes

1 Evans notes that a key moment in the formation of the New Homiletic was the civil rights movement as it gave wider exposure to the preaching found in African-American churches. Joseph Evans, 2008, 'The Black Folks' Blues and Jazz Hermeneutic', *Journal of Religious Thought*, 60, pp. 125–48, p. 139ff.

2 Among the five main contributors (Fred Craddock, David Buttrick, Eugene Lowry, Henry Mitchell and Charles Rice), only Mitchell, a key voice in African-American homiletics, does not fit that description. O. Wesley Allen (ed.), 2010, *The Renewed Homiletic*, Minneapolis: Fortress Press. p. 11.

3 A striking example of this can be found in David Buttrick's work where he writes that 'there are virtually no good reasons to talk about ourselves from the pulpit'. Buttrick has in view personal stories rather than personal speech but his argument reaches beyond personal illustrations and moves towards suggesting that the preacher does not fully own their own voice and experience. David Buttrick, 1987, *Homiletic Moves and Structures*, Philadelphia: Fortress, pp. 141–2.

4 Anthony Thiselton, 2019, *2 Corinthians: A Short Exegetical and Pastoral Commentary*, Eugene, OR: Cascade, pp.15–16.

5 2 Corinthians 11.11.

6 2 Corinthians 11.30.

7 Thiselton, *2 Corinthians*, p. 16.

8 Cf. Isaiah 64.8 and Lamentations 4.2.

9 These are the options suggested in the text and footnotes of the New Revised Standard Version.

10 Cf. Galatians 5.16–17. Dunn investigates the key Greek term *keta sarx*. James D. G. Dunn, 2006, *The Theology of Paul the Apostle*, Grand Rapids: Eerdmans, pp. 65–6.

11 Thiselton, *2 Corinthians*, p. 72.

12 Thiselton, *2 Corinthians*, p. 72.

13 Thiselton, *2 Corinthians*, pp. 72–3

14 Thiselton suggests that Rudolf Bultmann's approach devalues the importance of the historicity of Jesus. Like Davies, whom he quotes, Thiselton asserts that it is 'fleshly knowledge' which is repudiated, not a 'fleshly' Christ (Thiselton, *2 Corinthians*, p. 73).

15 Dunn, *The Theology of Paul the Apostle*, p. 482.

16 Cf. 2 Corinthians 1.22; Romans 8.9-11.

17 2 Corinthians 1.12.

18 As rendered, for example, by the interlinear Bible on the Bible Hub website here: https://biblehub.com/interlinear/2_corinthians/2-17.htm, accessed 13.4.21.

19 Cf. Romans 6.3–4 and see Dunn, *The Theology of Paul the Apostle*, especially pp. 390–412.

20 2 Corinthians 5.20.
21 These ideas are developed in Karl Barth, 1979, *Evangelical Theology: An Introduction*, Grand Rapids, MI: Eerdmans. An accessible summary of Barth's argument can be found in Stephen D. Morrison, 2017, *Karl Barth in Plain English*, Columbus, OH: Beloved, p. 42.
22 Barth, 1979, *Evangelical Theology*, p. 18.
23 This is argued well in Werner G. Jeanrond, 1991, *Theological Hermeneutics*, London: Macmillan, p. 129.
24 A good example of this is in Barth's correspondence with Adolf Van Harnack. A record of this, with some commentary, can be found in Keith L. Johnson, 2019, *The Essential Karl Barth: A Reader and Commentary*, Grand Rapids, MI: Baker, pp. 44–56.
25 Barth's doctrine of revelation shaped his approach to biblical interpretation; he famously wrote that 'The Word of God is God Himself in Holy Scripture … Scripture is holy and the Word of God as by the Holy Spirit it became and will become to the Church the witness of God's revelation'. Barth, as cited in G. W. Bromiley, 1955, 'Karl Barth's Doctrine of Inspiration', in *Journal of the Transactions of the Victoria Institute*, 87, pp. 66–80, p. 67.
26 Kevin J. Vanhoozer, 2006, 'A Person of the Book? Barth on Biblical Authority and Interpretation', in Sung Wook Chung (ed.), 2006, *Karl Barth and Evangelical Theology*, Milton Keynes: Paternoster, pp. 26–59, especially p. 34.
27 Barth placed such a high stock on proclamation in the church that he argued that all theology was primarily about sermon preparation. Barth's position is summarized by David Buttrick in the Foreword to Karl Barth, 1991, *Homiletics*, Louisville, KY: Westminster John Knox, p. 8.
28 Keith L. Johnson, 2010, *Karl Barth and the Analogia Entis*, Vol. 6, London: T&T Clark, p. 158.
29 Barth's position is explained in this way in Viazovski, Yaroslav, 2015, *Image and Hope: John Calvin and Karl Barth on Body, Soul, and Life Everlasting*, Princeton Theological Monograph Series Book 221, Kindle Edition, Eugene, OR: Pickwick, Location 4862 of 7540. In his *Church Dogmatics*, Barth himself wrote that 'it is not a being common to God and man [sic] which finally and properly establishes and upholds the fellowship between them, but God's grace'. This is cited in Johnson, *Karl Barth*, p. 158.
30 Keith Johnson explains Barth's position by comparing it to Emmanuel Hirsch in Johnson, *The Essential Karl Barth*, pp. 320–1.
31 Barth's position, which is outlined in his *Church Dogmatics*, is explored and cited in George Hunsinger, 1993, *How to Read Karl Barth*, Oxford: Oxford University Press, p. 98.
32 Johnson, *Karl Barth*, p. 161.

33 I have found the summary of Barth's position in this area to be particularly helpful in Johnson, *Karl Barth*, pp. 169–70.
34 Judges 21.25.
35 Barth, *Homiletics*, p. 44.
36 Barth, *Homiletics*, p. 49.
37 This follows Barth's explanation of his own position in Barth, *Homiletics*, pp. 44–5.
38 These ideas, which are explored in Barth's work, are summarized by Buttrick in his foreword to Barth, *Homiletics*, pp. 8–9.
39 Barth, as summarized by Buttrick in his foreword to Barth, *Homiletics*, p. 9.
40 See, for example, the excellent history of preaching offered by Alyce McKenzie, 2018, *Making a Scene in the Pulpit: Vivid Preaching for Visual Listeners*, Louisville, KY: Westminster John Knox, p. 12.
41 McKenzie, *Making a Scene*, pp. 33–4.
42 McKenzie, *Making a Scene*, pp. 33–4.
43 Keith Francis has written about the influence and popularity of preaching in between 1689 and 1901. He explains how sermons diversified and specialized for different contexts. See especially Keith A. Francis, 2012, *The Oxford Handbook of the British Sermon 1689–1901*, Oxford Handbooks, Oxford: Oxford University Press pp. 4–6.
44 Joel R. Beeke, 2008, *Living for God's Glory: An Introduction to Calvinism*, Kindle edition, Lake Mary, FL: Reformation Trust, Location 6449 of 9577.
45 Beeke, *Living for God's Glory*, Loc. 6449.
46 McKenzie, *Making a Scene*, p. 12.
47 A good example of this can be found in Peter Stevenson's explanation of developmental sermons, based on John Killinger's work, in Peter K. Stevenson, 2017, *SCM Studyguide to Preaching*, London: SCM Press, pp. 97–100.
48 Thiselton highlights the key contribution of Gerhard Ebeling and Ernst Fuchs to this movement. Anthony Thiselton, 1977, 'The New Hermeneutic', in I. Howard Marshall (ed.), *New Testament Interpretation: Essays on Principles and Methods*, Carlisle: Paternoster, pp. 308–33, esp. p. 328.
49 Allen notes the importance of the emerging thought about language in the twentieth century and points to Martin Heidegger and Ludwig Wittgenstein as key voices. (In O. Wesley Allen (ed.), 2010, *The Renewed Homiletic*, Minneapolis: Fortress, p. 5.)
50 For example, Walter Wink's famous declaration that the 'historical critical method is bankrupt' summed up the pervading sense that historical criticism fails to interpret Scripture in such a way that the past leads us to be changed in the here and now. Walter Wink, 1973, *The Bible in Human Transformation*, Minneapolis: Fortress, pp. 1–2.
51 Drawing on and developing the work of Hans-Georg Gadamer,

Thiselton offers a detailed exploration the horizons of the reader and the text in Anthony Thiselton, 1992, *New Horizons in Hermeneutics*, Grand Rapids, MI: Zondervan.

52 Stevenson offers a useful introduction to the three worlds of the text in Peter Stevenson, *Preaching*, pp. 25–55.

53 Paul Ricœur, 2008, *From Text to Action*, London: Continuum, p. 18.

54 This is explored by Wallace in M. I. Wallace, 1995, *The Second Naiveté*, Macon, Georgia: Mercer University Press, pp. xiii–xiv.

55 Thiselton, 'The New Hermeneutic', p. 328.

56 M. Monshau, 2018, 'The Influence of Pope Benedict XVI's Liturgical Initiatives on Preaching Beyond Postmodernity', in *Antiphon: A Journal for Liturgical Renewal*, 22(2), pp. 186–98, p. 187.

57 Fred Craddock, 2001, *As One Without Authority*, 4th edn, St Louis, MO: Chalice, pp. 6–14.

58 Craddock, *As One Without Authority*, pp. 22–3.

59 Thomas Long, 2016, *The Witness of Preaching*, Louisville, KY: Westminster John Knox, p. 116.

60 Long, *The Witness of Preaching*, p. 117.

61 Craddock builds here on the work of Barth who, in turn, had been influenced by Heidegger's later work on language. Craddock, *As One without Authority*, p. 35.

62 Craddock, *As One without Authority*, p. 35.

63 Craddock, *As One without Authority*, p. 106.

64 Craddock, *As One without Authority*, p. 92.

65 Allen shows these ideas about the eventfulness of sermons in the work of David Randolph, which preceded Craddock. The language of 'a happening' echoes the words of artist Allan Kaprow. (Allen, *The Renewed Homiletic*, pp. 7–8.)

66 Nigel J. Robb, 1999, *The Preaching Triangle*, Edinburgh: The Ministry Department of the Church of Scotland, p. 6.

67 Allen introduces the contribution of Harry Fosdick, R. E. C. Browne and H. Grady Davis as three examples of those whose work foreshadowed what was to come (Allen, *The Renewed Homiletic*, pp. 4–5).

68 F. Craddock, 1985, *Preaching*, Nashville, TN: Abingdon, p. 123.

69 Craddock, *Preaching*, p. 123.

70 Craddock, *As One without Authority*, p. 121.

71 McKenzie makes this point in McKenzie, *Making a Scene*, p. 12.

72 For a more detailed exploration see Allen, *The Renewed Homiletic*, pp. 8–9.

73 Craddock, *As One without Authority*, p. 45.

74 Allen, *The Renewed Homiletic*, p. 9.

75 Craddock, *As One without Authority*, p. 63.

76 Craddock, *As One without Authority*, p. 63.

THE PRESENT PREACHER

77 Craddock, *As One without Authority*, p. 63.
78 The ideas about language are explored in Allen, *The Renewed Homiletic*. p. 9. I think that Allen is deliberately using Barth's language where he rejects the idea that Word is ever 'brought home' on anything but its own terms. See Barth, *Evangelical Theology*, p. 182.
79 I have found Kate Bruce's *Igniting the Heart* to be an enormously helpful aid in exploring imagination in preaching. See in particular Bruce's summary of the sensory, intuitive, affective and intellectual functions of imagination in K. Bruce, 2015, *Igniting the Heart: Preaching and Imagination*, London: SCM Press, p. 28.
80 Craddock, *As One without Authority*, p. 65.
81 Craddock, *As One without Authority*, p. 65.
82 Craddock, *As One without Authority*, pp. 67–8.
83 McKenzie *Making a Scene*, p. 13.
84 Craddock, *As One without Authority*, pp. 99–100.
85 Craddock, *As One without Authority*, p. 44.
86 Craddock unpacks his thinking in this area in Craddock, *As One without Authority*, p. 44.
87 Craddock, *As One without Authority*, p. 44, emphasis mine.
88 Craddock explores counter-arguments to inductive preaching in Craddock, *As One without Authority*, pp. 55–7.
89 Craddock, *Preaching*, pp. 22–3.
90 Buttrick, *Homiletic*, pp. 22–8.
91 Buttrick, *Homiletic*, pp. 285–303, esp. p. 301.
92 Buttrick, *Homiletic*, p. 319.
93 Buttrick, *Homiletic*, p. 362.
94 Buttrick, *Homiletic*, p. 365.
95 Buttrick, *Homiletic*, p. 405.
96 E. Lowry, *The Homiletical Plot, expanded edition: the sermon as narrative art form*, Louisville, KY: Westminster John Knox Press, pp. 112–13.
97 Lowry, *The Homiletical Plot*, p. xxi.
98 Lowry, *The Homiletical Plot*, pp. 11–12.
99 Lowry, *The Homiletical Plot*, p. 26.
100 One example is the introduction of Walter Brueggemann's model of orientation-disorientation-reorientation in Stevenson, *Preaching*, pp. 68–70. Stevenson indicates that this approach has influenced a number of preachers, including Barbara Brown Taylor.
101 Lowry, *The Homiletical Plot*, pp. 71–2.
102 Craddock, *As One Without Authority*, p. 14.
103 Craddock, *As One Without Authority*, p. 14.
104 Shawn Radford offers a neat summary of the legacy of the New Homiletic in S. Radford, 2005, 'The New Homiletic within Non-Christendom', *Journal of the Evangelical Homiletics Society*, 5(2), pp. 4–18, especially p. 6.

105 For example, see Radford, 'The New Homiletic', or Timothy M. Slemmons, 'Between Text & Sermon: Philippians 3.17–4.1', *Interpretation: A Journal of Bible and Theology*, 64(1), (2010), pp. 78–80.
106 Radford, 'The New Homiletic', pp. 7–8.
107 Long, *Witness*, p. 49.
108 Long, *Witness*, pp. 20–1.
109 Long, *Witness*, p. 34.
110 Long, *Witness*, pp. 46–7.
111 Long, *Witness*, pp. 49–55.
112 Long, *Witness*, p. 52.
113 Long, *Witness*, p. 18.
114 Patrick Johnson offers a useful comparison of the theories of preaching offered by Thomas Long's *The Witness of Preaching*, David Lose's *Preaching in a Postmodern World* and Anna Carter Florence's *Preaching as Testimony* (Patrick Johnson, 2015, *The Mission of Preaching: Equipping the Community for Faithful Witness* Downers Grove, IL: InterVarsity Press, pp. 29–66).
115 Long, *Witness*, pp. 54–5.
116 Although McKenzie writes with the American context in view, it seems uncontroversial to draw these conclusions about the United Kingdom. McKenzie, *Making a Scene*, pp. 14–15.
117 McKenzie, *Making a Scene*, p. 23.
118 McKenzie, *Making a Scene*, p. 2.
119 McKenzie, *Making a Scene*, p. 81.
120 See, for example, Stevenson's chapter on episodic preaching in Stevenson, *Preaching*, pp. 118–30.
121 McKenzie, *Making a Scene*, p. 90.
122 McKenzie, *Making a Scene*, p. 26.
123 McKenzie, *Making a Scene*, pp. 32–3.
124 Taken from the Prayers at the Preparation of the Table for Easter from *Common Worship: Times and Seasons*, https://www.churchofengland.org/prayer-and-worship/worship-texts-and-resources/common-worship/churchs-year/times-and-seasons/easter#mmm211, accessed 13.4.21. Copyright © The Archbishops' Council 2006.
125 Helen Cameron discusses the work of the ARCS project and the four voices of theology which can be identified and attended to in theological reflection: espoused theology, operant theology, normative theology and formal theology (Helen Cameron, 'Life in all its Fullness: Engagement and Critique: Good News for Society.' *Practical Theology*, 5(1), (2012), pp. 11–26, p. 13.)
126 Long, *Witness*, p. ix.
127 Bonnie Miller-McLemore explains the methodology of practical theology in her introduction to Miller-McLemore, Bonnie J. (ed.), 2012, *The Wiley-Blackwell Companion to Practical Theology*, Oxford: Wiley-Blackwell, pp. 1–20, esp. p. 7.

128 For example, see Fiddes, P., 'Ecclesiology and ethnography: Two disciplines, two worlds?', in P. Ward (ed.), *Perspectives on Ecclesiology and Ethnography*, Grand Rapids, MI: Eerdmans. pp. 13–25, 19.

129 Elaine Graham, 2017, *Apologetics without Apology: Speaking of God in a World Troubled by Religion*, Didsbury Lecture Series Book, Eugene, OR: Cascade, p. 113.

130 2 Corinthians 4.13.

2

Present to God

LIZ SHERCLIFF

Present to God

I am increasingly convinced that those of us who have a preaching ministry are not called to prepare sermons, but to live a preaching life. This chapter is written from that conviction. By being present to God, I mean developing an awareness of God's presence, looking for God's activity, finding ways of understanding more of God through everyday life. In what follows we will explore how to live a preaching life, how to be present to God, in time, in whole-heartedness, in life's seasons and in practice – now. While I believe totally that great preachers are skilled wordsmiths, and that all preachers are called to be the church's poets; while I agree completely that exegesis of text and congregation are essential, I am also persuaded that among the vital qualities of good preachers is developing a preaching life. That will mean being a preacher all the time, in the 'now' – the sound of a Greensleeves jingle coming through my study window as I work reminds me that I am a preacher even in the ice cream queue!

As an adolescent my family attended a local Pentecostal church for several years. One Sunday the pastor told a story that has stayed with me ever since. It was probably apocryphal, but it makes an important point. One day, according to the pastor, he was called to visit a very sick man who had been in the congregation for years. 'I need you to get some papers out of that drawer,' the man said, pointing to a drawer across the room. 'What is it?' asked the pastor. 'It's my testimony,' came the reply. You can imagine the purpose of the sermon, although I cannot now remember that much: 'don't be a Christian who only has one experience of God, be a Christian all the time'. Theologically questionable as the premise of that sermon might be, it made an impression on my young mind. Now, years later, my favourite verse is 'The LORD is in this place – and I did not know it!' (Genesis 28.16). I do not mean that I assent to its truth, or that I take it as a reassuring thought in times of trouble, though both are true. I mean that it has been, in a whole variety of circumstances, a strength and a challenge to me: 'The Lord *is* in this place, but where?' Asking that kind of question is the work of being present to God and recognizing the now.

'Being present to God' means something like being constantly aware that 'my times are in your hand' (Psalm 31.15). That is, my past is with me now, my potential future is with me now, and I am present to God in holistic time. The writer of this Psalm is in a bad place, in distress, grief, sorrow. They have become the scorn of their enemies, they are like a broken vessel. And yet, the writer is able to say 'I trust in you Lord, my times are in your hand'. The same is true in good times, of course, though it seems to be a human failing that we forget God most easily when things are going well. Our times are in God's hand, God is all around us, being present to God means being aware of that.

'My times' are at the centre of the Psalmist's thinking in this verse. Time, or times, are at the centre of being present to God, too. In the years between the Psalmist writing and us reading those words, concepts of time have changed drastically. Although we speak confidently of time, and much of life is based on our use of time, nobody has properly defined it. Newton regarded it as a part of objective reality within which human beings exist. By contrast, Einstein argued that time is relative. As far back as the fifth century, St Augustine asked: 'What is time? Who can easily and briefly explain it? ... But what in speaking do we refer to more familiarly and knowingly than time?'[1]. We talk about time as though we know what it is, but actually we cannot define it, he says. Concepts of time are culturally and historically bound. In 2003 I was invited to speak at a women's breakfast conference in Kampala. My hosts emphasized the importance of starting and finishing on time. These were busy women, at least one would be expected in the Ugandan parliament later that morning. My European mind was prepared to start and finish speaking exactly at the appointed hour. But very few of the Ugandan delegates actually arrived punctually, and many didn't arrive until the scheduled finishing time. When I enquired what I should do, I was told just to wait until everyone had gathered, then to say what I had prepared. Punctuality and time both seemed to mean different things to me and to my hosts. I was well rooted in the view that regards time as a measurable, finite resource.

The invention of the clock, and later the digital clock, has allowed us to divide time into smaller and smaller units, and because we have divided it, we have the impression that we are in control of it. Before the invention of the clock, time was part of the natural cycle of life, marked out by the sun and moon. In Ancient Judaism and Islam the day was punctuated by regular prayer. The early Christians combined Jewish prayer practices with Roman hours, and divided the day into eight canonical hours, *Matins, Lauds, Prime, Terce, Sext, Nones, Vespers* and *Compline*. Only four services have numerical names, because the Romans only counted daylight hours. In monasteries monks were allocated to keeping watch through the night to ensure the community woke to pray. Mechanical clocks were first invented around 1300 CE. They were invented to support the prayer life of monastic communities, ensuring that they did not miss any of the offices. The first clocks, then, reminded people that time had a purpose – to worship God. Now, measurements of time are used to judge the length of sermons, decide how much time to allocate to particular tasks or agree when to meet together. Over several centuries we have moved from clocks being at our service, to clocks being in control of how we live.

Jesus' parable of the workers in the vineyard serves to illustrate attitudes to time (Matthew 20.1–16). 'The kingdom of heaven is like a landowner who went out early in the morning to hire labourers for his vineyard.' The landowner goes to the market four more times that day and each time hires some of those who had found no work. At the end of the day he pays each one the same. If we regard time as a commodity to buy and sell, we find it difficult to understand why those who only 'sold' a few hours of their time got the same as those who 'sold' a whole day. If, however, we regard time as purposeful, the parable takes on a different meaning. The workers who were not hired early are not standing idle in the sense of standing around with their hands in their pockets propping up walls. Rather, they are standing idle in the sense that a car engine is idle. They are turned on ready for the accelerator to be pushed so that they can spring into life. These idling workers are not shirkers, they are waiting for their day's purpose – another way of being present to God.

'God's time is holistic, all embracing, mysterious, and ever present'.[2] Being present to God means shifting our thinking from 'clock time' to 'holistic time'. In 'clock time' we make space in our days for 'Quiet Times', or for reading Morning Prayer. There are countless prayer and Bible reading schemes based on this approach to time. They are valuable, and important, just as the eight prayer times of the monastic day served an important purpose. But they are not the full story. In 'holistic time' everything is somehow together, rather than separate. The Bible does not clearly distinguish between past, present and future. Translators tell us that that is because of the language much of it is written in. But supposing that some of the confusion at least stems from the fact that time is 'all embracing' and 'ever present', that the Bible deals in 'holistic time' rather than 'clock time'? The matter of time caused misunderstanding between Jesus and his disciples. In John 11 Jesus' disregard for 'clock time' causes resentment when he does not rush to heal Lazarus, but waits two days. By the time Jesus arrives Lazarus has been dead four days. Jesus both mourns his friend (John 11.35) and intends to raise him from death. Perhaps hidden in the middle of the story is some explanation of how Jesus regards time. When Martha says 'I believe that you are the Messiah, the Son of God, the one coming into the world' (John 11.27), she seems to mean that the Messiah comes, is coming and will come. The coming of Jesus is not a once and for all event, but a constant coming (although of course his coming as God incarnate was once and for all). If we think about 'now' time, Jesus comes and has come. During lockdown my parish church held online Morning and Evening Prayer every day, and every day the person leading lit a candle, to remind us that Jesus *is* with us.

Perhaps our modern western 'clock time' paradigm affects how we read Paul's injunction to 'Pray in the Spirit at all times in every prayer and supplication' (Ephesians 6.18). In many churches, intercessions are introduced by a sentence something like 'in the power of the Spirit and in union with Christ'. The implication is that when we pray we invoke the power of the Spirit. If we translate the Greek of Ephesians 6.18 more literally, we might end up with something like 'through all prayer and supplication praying in every season in Spirit'. The emphasis in that case is not to invoke the Spirit when we pray, but to pray, be present to God, in every season in Spirit.

The separation of past, present and future encouraged by 'clock time' is a false division of time. The past is not gone and the future is not only yet to come; both exist only because in the present we bring them to mind. Some time ago, I went to Evensong at St Paul's Cathedral in London. I was very struck by the words used to introduce the service. 'You have not come simply to worship,' the minister said, 'you have come to join in the stream of worship rising from this place for centuries.' In other words, worship here is bigger than you. 'Holistic time' makes us part of an all-embracing time, in which ever-present others are a part.

A while ago now, given that working practices changed significantly in March 2020, I heard a colleague in the office humming the hymn 'Tell me the old, old story'. Immediately, I was transported to a plain hall, furnished with the kind of chair that is constructed from tubular metal and strung with burgundy canvas that seemed particularly designed to encourage short sermons, or at least provoke a profound desire for them. It was where the local Pentecostal Church met when I was in my teens. We used to sing that hymn regularly. Along with the memory came the names and faces of some of those who sat around us. In addition, though, there came flooding back the memories of why we were there and the attendant emotions. My family, other than my grandfather, who was an avowed atheist until the day he fell off a roof and prayed on the way down, were Anglican. We attended the nearest evangelical Anglican church morning, afternoon and evening on a Sunday, and were so much a part of it that my sister and I also went to the associated school despite its not being our nearest. It all changed when my father left us to set up home with someone else. The vicar supported my mother's application for a divorce. But once she was divorced she was barred from communion. And so we ended up at the local Pentecostal church, singing hymns like 'Tell me the old, old story' on a Sunday. Also into my mind came images and sounds from a *Praise Baby DVD*,[3] something that helped my grandchildren get to sleep when they were babies. Thinking of them brought to mind the length of the pandemic lockdown and when I might get to see them again. Past and future together in an instant, all from the presently sung lines of an old hymn! That, I think, is something like 'holistic time', a consciousness of all that is forming me now.

Being present to God in whole-heartedness

The Bible places the heart at the centre of who we are and what we do:

> I will give thanks to the LORD with my whole heart;
> I will tell of all your wonderful deeds. (Psalm 9.1)

> Create in me a clean heart, O God. (Psalm 51.10)

> My flesh and my heart may fail,
> but God is the strength of my heart
> and my portion for ever. (Psalm 73.26)

Trust in the LORD with all your heart. (Proverbs 3.5)

Keep your heart with all vigilance,
for from it flow the springs of life. (Proverbs 4.23)

For out of the heart come evil intentions, murder, adultery, fornication, theft, false witness, slander. (Matthew 15.19)

For where your treasure is, there your heart will be also. (Luke 12.34)

Set your affection [heart] on things above, not on things on the earth. (Colossians 3.2 KJV)

One of the striking things about these verses is the number of times intentionality is implied – 'I will', 'trust', 'keep', 'set'. The psalmist has determined to do these things. Intentionality is different from intent. Intentionality gets things done, intent intends to! Intentionality involves purpose and focus. Being intentionally present to God means more than hoping that we might realize God is present. It means being vigilant, putting our trust, setting our affections. In short, it requires wholeheartedness.

People of many faiths and of none testify to the benefits of *still*-heartedness, 'mindfulness'; even the NHS promotes it as a means of dealing with stress. Mindfulness involves sitting still and paying attention to what is going on, within and without; our thoughts and feelings, the sounds that surround us. Mindfulness might be part of still-heartedness, but still-heartedness goes beyond it, because still-heartedness involves becoming aware of God, not just of self. Where mindfulness asks 'where am I?' still-heartedness asks 'where is God?' We can be still-hearted in the midst of life's storms, as the poem below, written during Storm Doris in 2017, serves to illustrate:

Weather Bomb

Along the lakeside
the storm bellows
waves break
wind howls
feet splash
through endless, edgeless puddles.
Along the lakeside
my heart is stilled
and I find You.

Along the lakeside
the storm bellows
emails to answer
papers to read
sermons to prepare
tasks to complete
feet splash
through endless, edgeless puddles.
Along the lakeside
my mind is stilled
and I find You.
(© Liz Shercliff, 2017)

Still-heartedness is an intentional recognition that 'my flesh and my heart may fail, but God is the strength of my heart [stillness] and portion for ever' (Psalm 73.26). In still-heartedness every aspect of our being comes together in wholeness.

As we have seen, the Hebrew and Christian scriptures place the heart at the centre of all personal life as motivator of thoughts and actions. The Hebrew words often translated 'perfect' or 'blameless' in our Old Testament (*kol* – the whole, all; *lebab* – the inner being, mind, will, heart) might better be translated 'wholehearted'. Perfection and blamelessness imply something about morality, or behaviour, where wholeheartedness relates more to intentionality. Thus, Proverbs 2.21 says the upright will abide in the land and the *wholehearted* will remain in it, and Proverbs 28.10 says the *wholehearted* will have a goodly inheritance.

What do I mean by wholeheartedness? I have in mind the kind of people Brené Brown, professor, researcher and author, discovered during her research on shame. She describes them as people 'living and loving with their whole hearts',[4] and characterizes them as people who cultivate authenticity; self-compassion; a resilient spirit; gratitude and joy; intuition and trusting faith; creativity, play and rest; calm and stillness; meaningful work; laughter, song and dance. Turning toward these things means turning away from others, and here I hope the link between wholeheartedness and 'holistic time' will become apparent. To live wholeheartedly, according to Brown, means letting go of what other people think; of perfectionism; of feeling powerless; of the need for certainty; of comparison; of the drive for productivity and busyness; of anxiety; of 'ought to'; and of the need to be in control. 'Clock time' encourages our drive for productivity and busyness, it drives our need to be in control, it lulls us into thinking we must spend time productively. Wholeheartedness, then, encourages us toward holistic time, and away from clock time. Wholeheartedness allows us to take Sabbath, a practice that encourages us to simply be, now, rather than worry about achievement.

Compare these values to Paul's definition of love in 1 Corinthians 13. Below is Tom Wright's translation, but I have taken the liberty of reinterpreting the first line:

Love is wholehearted, love is kind
knows no jealousy, makes no fuss,
is not puffed up, has no shameless ways,
doesn't force its rightful claim:
doesn't rage, or bear a grudge,
doesn't cheer at others' harm,
rejoices, rather, in the truth.
Love bears all things, believes all things;
love hopes all things, endures all things.
Love never fails ...[5]

Both what Brené Brown says and what St Paul writes make clear that wholehearted living focuses on now. There is no anxiety about the future – no forcing of rightful claims; not hanging on to the past, no grudges. Wholeheartedness means looking at where we are, standing in love and hope.

Being present to God in season and out

Life at the beginning of the twenty-first century in the Western world is largely unaffected by seasonal changes. We might, if we are observant, note the new life of Spring, the warmth of Summer, the plenty of early Autumn, and the earth's Winter sleep, but largely we carry on regardless. Artificial light and heat mean we are not dependent on the sun. Modern farming and shopping mean we are at least one step removed from the production of our food. Simlarly, the eight seasons of the church's year go unmarked in some churches also. Yet, they are useful. Advent looks forward, and is a time for reflection, penitence and rejoicing; Christmas begins the story of Jesus; Epiphany is a time of inclusion, also subtitled in the Book of Common Prayer 'The Manifestation of Christ to the Gentiles'; Lent is a period of increased prayer and self-examination; Holy Week runs the gamut of human emotion, from the triumph of Palm Sunday through betrayal, intimacy, agony and death; Ascension reminds us, as a pastor at one of the Pentecostal churches of my youth shouted, arms raised 'there's a man in the heavenlies'; Pentecost celebrates the coming of the Holy Spirit, the life of the Church; the Transfiguration reminds us that Jesus is both human and divine, a mystery. Having spent much of my Christian life in churches of a particular persuasion, I am only lately coming to appreciate the Church's seasons. While we nodded in the direction of Advent, Christmas, Easter and Pentecost, Lent and Holy Week were barely acknowledged. Even on Good Friday the preacher could not resist proclaiming that 'Sunday is coming'. We missed the dark times, the times when God seems far away, or when we know ourselves unworthy. Our worship constantly looked ahead to more cheery times. Ignoring the harder times is one way in which churches seek to dispel the dark seasons of life too quickly. It's a way of assigning to God's people long ago, rather than accepting for ourselves, the words of Isaiah 45.3:

> I will give you the treasures of darkness
> and riches hidden in secret places,
> so that you may know that it is I, the LORD,
> the God of Israel, who call you by your name.

During Holy Week 2020 the country was in a national lockdown caused by the covid pandemic. The Old Testament readings somehow seemed particularly appropriate. The reading for Tuesday was from Lamentations 3 and included the words 'God has brought me into darkness without any light ... he has made me sit in darkness'. My first response to the reading involved turning on a metaphorical light: 'God has brought us this far and God will see us through'. But the text goes further than that. '*God has brought me into* darkness ... *God has made me sit in* darkness'. It is not, according to Lamentations, that we find ourselves in darkness and God is with us there – God brings us to it. Reflecting on the text brought me to John of the Cross, who regarded darkness as God's best gift, intended for our liberation. God puts *out* our lights to keep us safe, he said. We are never more in danger of stumbling than when we think we know where we are going. But when we can no longer see the road ahead, when we can no longer read the map we brought with us, and we can no longer sense anything around us that might guide us through the dark. Then and only then do we allow ourselves to rely solely on God's protection. The only thing the dark night requires of us is to remain fully aware, to stay in that very moment in which God seems most absent. The night will do the rest. Rather than look ahead for a glimpse of light, or look back to when things seemed better, John of the Cross encourages to live now, present to God, even though it is dark.

There are treasures to be found in dark places that we never see if we insist on looking only at the light. In her amazing book *Learning to Walk in the Dark*, Barbara Brown Taylor writes:

> There is a divine presence that transcends all your ideas about it, along with all your language for calling it to your aid, which is not above using darkness as the wrecking ball that brings all your false gods down – but whether you decide to trust the witness of those who have gone before you, or you decide to do whatever it takes to become a witness yourself, here is the testimony of faith: darkness is not dark to God; the night is as bright as the day.[6]

Rather than dispel the darkness as quickly as possible, living a preaching life might require us to learn from, and be formed by, the God who is in darkness as much as in light.

As well as lunar, or Church seasons, lives have their own seasons. There are dry seasons and fruitful seasons; seasons where we flourish and seasons where we wither. God is in each of these, and each has potential to develop a deeper understanding of God. Preachers who orient themselves according to their life season will be able to share deeper wisdom, instead of insisting that the old wisdom should fit, even though it clearly doesn't. Reading some of the language in 1 Peter in light of the apostle Peter's experience of failure and betrayal as well as in light of his first-hand knowledge of Jesus surely gives his words greater depth:

> being protected by the power of God through faith for a salvation ready to be revealed in the last time. In this you rejoice, even if now for a little while you have had to suffer various trials, so that the genuineness of your faith – being more precious than gold that, though perishable, is tested by fire – may be found to result in praise and glory and honor when Jesus Christ is revealed (1 Peter 1.5–7).

> When he was abused, he did not return abuse; when he suffered, he did not threaten; but he entrusted himself to the one who judges justly. He himself bore our sins in his body

on the cross, so that, free from sins, we might live for righteousness; by his wounds you have been healed.[25] For you were going astray like sheep, but now you have returned to the shepherd and guardian of your souls (1 Peter 2.23–25).

Collectively, nationally and globally, since early 2020 we have all gone through an unprecedented life-season. For some it has been a period of grief, for others of loneliness and purposelessness, and for others of frantic, necessary activity as work and home-schooling had to be accommodated into the days that did not have the needed elasticity.

Culturally, politically, globally and locally, we live through seasons. Following the story of God's people in the Old Testament, we can identify seasons of journeying, of exodus, of oppression and of liberation. Alongside these the Bible traces the development of how God's people speak of God, how what they learn from life-experience informs their theology. In the Old Testament, the idea of God as King was developed after the Israelites had a human king. The early church used existing ideas about Caesar to describe Jesus – 'the "gospel" was the good news of Caesar's having established peace and security for the world', so when Jesus' followers said the same about Him, they were borrowing ideas from elsewhere.[7] Saying 'Jesus is Lord' in the first century also implied 'Caesar is not'.

It is important to recognize the season we are in not simply to find metaphors and illustrations, but also so that we can be present *for* God as well as *to* God. At the start of my ordination training I was invited with others to visit an A level RE class. The brief was to speak to the group about why we were Christians. The first trainee minister to speak said what she thought was a quite simple sentence: 'I became a Christian when I realized that Jesus died for my sins.' There was silence. Then one of the girls raised her hand and asked 'Who did what for your what?' The trainee minister had not oriented herself according to the season we were in, and hence completely failed to communicate. God, I suspect, was more in the student's question than in the words chosen as 'testimony'.

To be called to preach is to be called to see the world as clearly and honestly as we can. It involves an ongoing attempt, in the words of Burns, 'To see ourselves as others see us', but it also requires a willingness to see what others see, not to look away from poverty or suffering or injustice or privilege.[8]

As I wrote this I wondered what the challenge of Doug Gay's words might mean for my next sermon. I was preaching on the first Sunday of 2021, as what had been a very difficult year for the world drew to an end, but what might be an equally difficult year began. My research into others' sermons revealed a preponderance of positivism – God had been revealed in the kindness of neighbours to one another; there was hope now that we had a vaccine. Was such relentless optimism really what people wanted from their preacher? Did it reflect what I saw when I heard of cancelled operations leading to serious illness or death? Preaching in season requires honesty that can be painful for us and for our hearers too, so we must learn to find God in the world's realities, not just in wishful thinking.

Being present to God in practice

What actions or habits might we develop in order to live preaching lives, to be present to God in time, in wholeheartedness and in season?

Two images, I think, are helpful: beachcombing and playing. I will need to define each before we move on. For our purposes here, beachcombing includes adventuring, noticing and pilgrimage; play includes experiment, imagination and purpose. Living a preaching live means all of these things, every day.

Beachcombing

Good beachcombers find everything from worthless bits of litter to sea glass from which jewellery can be made. The first requisite of good beachcombing is looking at the ground you are standing on. I first learnt of the spiritual value of this practice from Barbara Brown Taylor's book *An Altar in the World*:

> No one longs for what he or she already has, and yet the accumulated insight of those wise about the spiritual life suggests that the reason so many of us cannot see the red X that marks the spot is because we are standing on it. The treasure we seek requires no lengthy expedition, no expensive equipment, no superior aptitude or special company. All we lack is the willingness to imagine that we already have everything we need. The only thing missing is our consent to be where we are.[9]

Beachcombers do not wish to be elsewhere, they focus on what is around them. Preachers who practice beachcombing preach sermons that resonate with hearers. What they say didn't happen a long time ago or a long way away, it might have been just round the corner!

At the same time, beachcombing requires inquisitiveness. Whole shells can only be picked out from among broken ones if the beachcomber stops, stoops and stares. Exodus 3 illustrates the value of inquisitiveness. Moses, on the run from Egypt because he killed a slave-master there, is in the wilderness caring for his father-in-law's flock. He notices a burning bush. Burning bushes in the wilderness are not uncommon.[10] What is important in the story is that Moses goes beyond noticing. He stops what he is doing to stare at 'this great sight' (Exodus 3.3). He goes over to the bush to find out what is happening. And 'when the LORD saw that he had turned aside to see, God called to him' (Exodus 3.4). God responds to Moses' inquisitiveness and calls to him from the bush. The ground becomes holy because of Moses' curiosity. Just as inquisitiveness leads to Moses to standing on holy ground, so I believe preachers' inquisitiveness leads to us standing on holy ground as we speak to our congregations. Moses' inquisitiveness leads to a moment of revelation, calling and promise: 'I am the God of your father, the God of Abraham, the God of Isaac, and the God of Jacob ... I will send you ... I will be with you' (Exodus

3.6, 10, 12). There is probably no such thing as a preacher who does not want to experience revelation, call and promise from God!

Beachcombing leads us to find unexpected things in unexpected places – God, now, where we are. Sometimes we fail to see God here, because our vision is too fixed. We will always see what we expect to see unless we look closely at where we are – the text will always say what the text has always said unless we read it with care. One way of starting is to look at everyone present in the story, and whether or not they appear in our preaching. Take, for example, John's account of the wedding at Cana (John 2). A recent book on preaching offers four ways of using this particular biblical passage, at a wedding, at a prayer meeting, in an address to Christian workers and to a local congregation (with non-Christians present). All four focus on Jesus and treat the others in the story as bit-parts. They are there to demonstrate the preacher's point that we should bring problems to Jesus, as Mary did; go to Jesus with our needs, and also our friends' needs, as Mary did; be used by Jesus, as Mary was; think of Jesus as a sign of new wine.[11] There is nothing intrinsically wrong with any of those messages, except that once the sermon begins most experienced congregations will know exactly where it is headed. Interpreting the passage in this way ignores some key people – Mary, the servants, the steward, even perhaps the bride and groom. The beachcombing preacher might wonder what contributions they make to our understanding of God and God's Son. Mary, for example, takes authority both over the servants and over Jesus himself. She has been dismissed by her son, and yet she instructs the servants to do as he says and, in my mind at least, then looks over at Jesus with a 'get out of that' expression on her face. Does she prompt Jesus to launch his ministry, because like the rest of us, Jesus needed someone to have confidence in him? What about the servants? They must have known how much trouble might ensue if they poured out water into the steward's cup, yet they somehow believed, on the instruction of a woman, that they ought to do it. What might we say about the discerning steward, or the blissfully unaware wedding couple?

Beachcombing preaching means that texts do not always have to say what they have always said, there are new gems to be found. Beachcombing opens up divine possibilities.

Playing

Play for the preacher involves playing with ideas and words primarily, although it also might involve the kind of play where there is risk. In the Gospels, Jesus many times says: 'You have heard it said ... but I say.' Jesus uses the word *amar*, which means 'interpret', in these instances, and so is really saying: '[it] has been interpreted like that, but I interpret [it] like this'. In Matthew 19.17, for example, 'And he said to him, "Why do you ask me about what is good? There is only one who is good. If you wish to enter into life, keep the commandments".' Jesus is really asking: 'Why do you interpret "good" the way you do?' This is an essential question for inquisitive preachers: 'Why do I interpret this in the way I am doing?' We will look more closely at this question in a later chapter, but for now it is important to say that unless we are inquisitive enough to wonder why we interpret things the way we do, and to play with new possibilities, we cannot be present to God *now*. Let's be clear that play is structured and ordered in many of its definitions: theatre plays have lines; sport has rules; instruments have techniques. Play is purposeful, it's how we find out what is possible and what is not.

Playing with ideas was certainly not part of my early Christian experience. Life was presented, by my youth group leaders and by many speakers at university Christian Union meetings, as an exercise something like painting by numbers. God had pre-ordained how I was meant to paint each aspect of my life, and I just had to find the right colour and apply it in the right way. Verses that seemed to speak of God's advance planning were quoted regularly, and often to good effect. I felt guilty if I wasn't sure what to do, and anxious that failing to find the right paint pot would lead to my eternal damnation.

My saving grace, in many ways, was my mother. Being in a church that extolled not only the need to discern 'God's will', but also the value of marriage, as a divorcee she was in a potentially tricky position. Fortunately, she was well acquainted with Jeremiah 18, the story of the potter's house:

> The word that came to Jeremiah from the LORD: 'Come, go down to the potter's house, and there I will let you hear my words.' So I went down to the potter's house, and there he was working at his wheel. The vessel he was making of clay was spoiled in the potter's hand, and he reworked it into another vessel, as seemed good to him.
> Then the word of the Lord came to me: Can I not do with you ...? (Jeremiah 18.1–6)

I began to see that God does not present us with painting-by-numbers kits, but with a blank canvas and an array of beautiful colours. The canvas has boundaries, of course, but there is no limit to our creativity.

Playing with ideas is an important aspect of theology, and of preaching. Kate Bruce sums up the approach that I adopt in Bible reading and preaching:

> If we see revelation as fixed and finished, the task of the preacher is to extract the meaning from the text and teach it. This leads to an account of preaching that is overly rational, takes no account of genre, nor the context of the preacher's life, nor the situation of the hearers.[12]

If you have espoused the rationalistic view of Bible reading and preaching you will be suspicious of the imagination, perhaps because you equate it with fanciful thinking. Preachers and writers from quite different theological positions focus on God's imagination in creation, however. In the late 1990s, Tony Campolo preached in Manchester. Dwelling on God's creative activity, he imagined God making a daisy, and enjoying it so much the Almighty kept on saying 'again, again'. Perhaps more academically, Donal O'Leary wrote:

Divine imagination is wider and wilder than we could ever dream of, and it is closer and more loving than we dare hope. God's imagination is at work in every aspect of creation from the heart of the cosmos to the heart of the tiniest insect and in the very core of our own being.[13]

Lack of imagination disables our understanding of ourselves and of others. Without imagination there is neither empathy nor compassion. Without imagination sermons can become dry instruction or relentless scolding.

As a witness to God's activity in the world we are called not 'to testify in the abstract but to find just those words and patterns that can convey the event the witness has seen and heard'.[14] Finding the right words involves playing with words, finding patterns, communicating experiences that chime with the words in our set Bible text, or that evoke similar thoughts and feelings. 'Finding just those words' is an important skill. Preachers are the Church's wordsmiths, preachers are called to use language well. Words are our most important tool, as St Ambrose said, 'it did not suit God to save his people through logic'.[15] Pinning down doctrine, or biblical ideas in a sermon, rather than using imagination to let them fly, is rather like Alastair Reid's description of defining birds: 'say the soft bird's name but do not be surprised to see it fall'.[16] Naming the bird 'straking the harbour water and then plummeting' is unimportant in comparison with 'the amazement of its rising', the poet says. The daily task of the preacher, in a world where words have been devalued by fake truth and political tweets, is:

> searching for words that listen, words that hear the pulse, words that read between the lines, words that distil, words that distrust first impressions, words from which we can't retreat, words of receptive insight, words without razor blades in them, with no chemical additives but with some natural nutrients, words that help us migrate towards the things that matter, words that dispel illusions without leaving us disillusioned.[17]

If words are the essential device in our preacher's toolbox, it makes sense that living a preaching life involves honing and maintaining them. It means spending time reading, listening and experimenting with words. Dylan Thomas wrote of falling in love with words, Mark Oakley wrote of the splash of words.[18] Words used well bring God near – hence in Mark's Gospel we are told 'Jesus came ... preaching' (Mark 1.14, KJV). Words can close things down or open them up. A neatly argued, three-point sermon presents to the congregation a finished-off pill of truth they simply need to swallow. Leaving loose ends, floating ideas, unresolved chords gives the congregation something to work with the following week. For that reason, I resist ending a sermon with the word 'Amen'. I am happy to leave a time of quiet, for the congregation to be unsure even whether the sermon has finished – for in reality, it hasn't, until they take it and make of it what they will.

One of the biggest obstacles in the way of any Christian learning is, according to John Hull, the need to be a pilgrim, which includes the need to be creative with the Creator.[19] As a preacher it is all too easy to imagine that Hull's observation applies to the congregation, without also applying it to myself. Preachers' learning too needs to be informed by pilgrimage and imagination. If that means that we speak more tentatively, and with less unassailable authority, that can only be a good thing. As Tom Long writes, people 'are less and less impressed by preachers who present the Christian faith as a finished business',[20] and more interested in sermons as shared journeying.

Beachcombing and play, then, can help us find God in places we might not have found God before. Combined they can open new potential for preaching too.

Abiding in God

Culture changes theology in subtle ways, even in the keenest of preachers. At the end of a lecture for clergy, one of the attendees asked me: 'Where is God in all this?' It transpired that he was basically ticking me off for not being clear that sermon preparation should start with saying a prayer. My question back, though, was: 'Where did God go?' One way or another, the conversation got around to the word 'abide'. My questioner saw abiding in God as something we slip in and out of, and above all, somewhere where we are still. I suspected that this theology came more from popular culture than it did from Jesus' words in John 15. The hymn 'Abide with Me' is played by the orchestra as the ship goes down in the film *Titanic*. For football fans the hymn has been synonymous with the FA cup final since it replaced *Alexander's Ragtime Band* in 1927. The words, though, are misleading. They ask God to abide with us in life's difficulties, and 'in life, in death', when 'other helpers fail, and comforts flee', the request is that God remain 'at hand'. If we have to ask God to be with us in those times, the implications is that either God is not around at other times, or that we don't need the divine presence when things are going swimmingly. Neither is true.

By contrast, Jesus speaks of abiding in terms of mutuality:

> Abide in me as I abide in you. Just as the branch cannot bear fruit by itself unless it abides in the vine, neither can you unless you abide in me. I am the vine, you are the branches. Those who abide in me and I in them bear much fruit, because apart from me you can do nothing. Whoever does not abide in me is thrown away like a branch and withers; such branches are gathered, thrown into the fire, and burned. If you abide in me, and my words abide in you, ask for whatever you wish, and it will be done for you. (John 15.4–7)

It is not possible to separate the vine from its branches. Viniculturists will know the importance of tending vines, by pruning and grafting. Even branches that are thrown into the fire remain vines, they are simply dead vines. Abiding means both abiding in God and God abiding in us, now.

Living a preaching life is likewise mutual. It is noticing where and how Jesus abides in us, as well as intentionally abiding in him. Our tools, as preachers, are imagination, observation and words. Tom Long proposes that the preacher should be a witness whose authority comes from what they have seen and heard.[21] To preach authentically that God is always with us, we need to see and hear God speak in our everyday lives.

Martin Luther, speaking of all vocations in life, said this:

> Only look at your tools, your needle, your thimble, your beer barrel, your articles of trade, your scales, your measures, and you will find this saying written on them. You will not be able to look anywhere where it does not strike your eyes. None of the things with which you deal daily are too trifling to tell you this incessantly, if you are but willing to hear it; and there is no lack of such preaching, for you have as many preachers as there are transactions, commodities, tools and other implements in your house and estate.[22]

Returning to the story I told at the start of this chapter, about the old man wanting to retrieve his testimony from a drawer, I conclude the chapter with a different story, one from Barbara Brown Taylor:

> Many years ago now, a wise old priest invited me to come speak at his church in Alabama.
> 'What do you want me to talk about?' I asked him.
> 'Come tell us what is saving your life now,' he answered. It was as if he had swept his arm across a dusty table and brushed all the formal china to the ground. I did not have to try to say correct things that were true for everyone. I did not have to use theological language that conformed to the historical teachings of the church. All I had to do was figure out what my life depended on. All I had to do was figure out how I stayed as close to that reality as I could, and then find some way to talk about it that helped my listeners figure out those same things for themselves. [23]

Just as I am ... I come

You will have gathered by now that during my early years my mother, sister and I attended a variety of churches. For a time we went to The Salvation Army. The band regularly played a hymn that struck deep chords with me: 'Just as I am ... O Lamb of God, I come'. That sums up one aspect of being present to God – it is necessary to 'come'. But how, and what does that mean?

The Bible gives us some helpful indicators about being present to God. In Genesis 18, God visits Abraham and Sarah on the plains of Mamre to remind them that they will have a son. Sarah isn't around to hear the word from God direct, she has to go and cook the food. But she does overhear God's promise to her husband. Sometimes, I wonder whether that is as close as I get to hearing God speak – overhearing what is said to others. For Samuel, in 1 Samuel 3, God speaks more clearly. God speaks so clearly, in fact, that Samuel imagines it's Eli the priest shouting him. But once the confusion is identified, Samuel prepares himself, and when the Lord arrives, Samuel says: 'Speak, for your servant is listening.' Choosing a place where we can ready ourselves to hear from God might prove a helpful habit.

For Elijah, God's voice comes differently. Elijah has just seen off the prophets of Baal, he's exhausted and runs away to be by himself. God first of all feeds him, then listens to him, and finally God comes to the prophet in sheer silence (a still small voice), and offers a challenge: 'What do you think you are doing?' (1 Kings 19.7–17) – a great preacher's question, as we will see in the next chapter. Sometimes we need to come as we are, possibly pretty wretched, and allow God to restore us.

Luke 8.40–56 has two contrasting prayers. Jairus falls at Jesus' feet praying for his dying daughter. He knows what he wants, and feels confident to ask. The outcast woman, who has been ill for years, simply reaches out.

Overhearing God, listening for God, allowing God to minister to us, praying for others, and simply reaching out are all ways of being present to God, now. But what might we practically do? Looking out for God's work in others is no bad thing, particularly if, like Sarah, we might be a part of the divine purpose. People we work with, care about, share our lives with might all hear from God about something that impacts us. More personally, though, telling God we want to hear, or being honest about how we feel; laying out our issues in words, or mental images, or writing in a journal; holding something before God.

Becoming quiet and still

Stilling prayer, or simply mindfulness, encourages us to sit with a straight back, plant our feet on the floor and rest our hands, palms up, on our knees; to become aware of our breathing, and of our bodies, and to acknowledge distractions. In a busy household these might not be possible, of course. We might use repetition of words as a way of focusing our minds – repeating the Jesus Prayer until our minds and hearts are still, for example (this uses the words: 'Lord Jesus Christ, Son of God, have mercy on me'). Rosaries and holding-crosses are useful ways of focusing too, as is using Lectio Divina, which I invite you to do below.

Thomas Cranmer graphically exhorted his hearers to 'chew the cud, that we may have sweet juice, spiritual effect, marrow, honey, kernel, taste, comfort and consolation'.[24] A former Abbot of Worth Abbey explains lectio like this:

- 'The text is seen as a gift to be received, not a problem to be dissected ... let the text come to you.'
- 'In order to receive what the text has to offer we must read slowly.'
- 'Before reading pray that God will speak to you through the text. During reading, allow the reading to evolve into meditation and then into prayer and finally contemplation. When the reading is concluded, keep some phrase in mind and repeat it throughout the day so that prayerful reading becomes prayerful living.'

I have often used this as a means of beginning sermon preparation. Why not look at the Lectionary Gospel for next Sunday and prepare a sermon using this method?

> ## A Form of Lectio Divina
>
> *You may want to come back to this at a more convenient time.*
>
> Sit comfortably, straight, with your feet flat on the ground.
> Breathe deeply.
> Ask God to speak to you through the passage you are about to read.
>
> > In the morning, while it was still very dark, he got up and went out to a deserted place, and there he prayed. And Simon and his companions hunted for him. When they found him, they said to him, 'Everyone is searching for you.' He answered, 'Let us go on to the neighbouring towns, so that I may proclaim the message there also; for that is what I came out to do." And he went throughout Galilee, preaching. (Mark 1.35–39; NRSV has 'proclaiming the message')
>
> Does a word or phrase attract your attention? Dwell here until you discern God's word for today, for you, here.
> Read the passage again. How does it speak to you?
> Read it again. What are you being called to do?

Questions for further reflection

- How is your passion for God reflected in your preaching?
- Imagine you were invited to speak on a secular radio show because you were a Christian and a preacher. If the interviewer asked you: 'How do you make time for God in your sermon preparation?', how would you respond (without using theological jargon)?
- If your spiritual director or soul friend asked you the same question, how might you respond differently?

Notes

1 L. Manning, D. Cassel and J. C. Cassel, 2013, 'St. Augustine's Reflections on Memory and Time and the Current Concept of Subjective Time in Mental Time Travel', *Behavioral Sciences (Basel, Switzerland)*, 3(2), pp. 232–43. https://doi.org/10.3390/bs3020232, accessed 13.4.21.

2 J. Swinton, 2017, *Becoming Friends of Time: Disability, Timefullness, and Gentle Discipleship*, London: SCM Press, p. 15.

3 *The Praise Baby Collection*, Franklin, TN: Big House Kids.

4 B. Brown, 2010, *The Gifts of Imperfection*, Kindle Edition, Center City, Minnesota: Hazelden, Location 138.

5 Tom Wright, 2010, *Virtue Reborn*, London: SPCK, p. 156.

6 Barbara Brown Taylor, 2014, *Learning to Walk in the Dark*, Kindle Edition, Norwich: Canterbury Press, Location 217.

7 R. A. Horsley, 2002, *Jesus and Empire: The Kingdom of God and the New World*, Minneapolis: Fortress Press, p. 66.

8 Doug Gay, 2018, *God be in My Mouth: 40 Ways to Grow as a Preacher*, Edinburgh: St Andrew Press, p. 19.

9 Barbara Brown Taylor, 2009, *An Altar in the World: Finding the Sacred Beneath our Feet*, Norwich: Canterbury Press, pp. xiv–xv.

10 Joe Schwarez of McGill University, among other researchers, nominates the *Dictamnus albus* plant, also known as the gas plant. It exudes a range of volatile oils that readily catch fire. The problem with the theory is that the oils need a spark in order to ignite, and they don't burn for long.

11 Timothy Keller, 2015, *Preaching: Communicating Faith in an Age of Scepticism*, London: Hodder and Stoughton, pp. 299–300.

12 K. Bruce, 2015, *Igniting the Heart: Preaching and Imagination*, London: SCM Press, pp. 38–9.

13 D. O'Leary, 2006, *Imagination: The Forgotten Dimension*, The Furrow, p. 525.

14 T. Long, 2005, *The Witness of Preaching*, second edition, Louisville: Westminster John Knox Press, p. 14.

15 M. Oakley, 2019, *By Way of the Heart: The Seasons of Faith*, Norwich: Canterbury Press, p. xx.

16 A. Reid, 1958, *Growing Flying Happening*, The New Yorker.

17 M. Oakley, *By Way of the Heart*, p. xix.

18 M. Oakley, 2016, *The Splash of Words: Believing in Poetry*, Norwich: Canterbury Press.

19 J. Hull, 2011, *What Prevents Christian Adults from Learning?* London: SCM Press.

20 T. G. Long, 2005, 'The Distance We Have Traveled: Changing Trends in Preaching', in Day, David, Astley, J., and Francis, L. J., *A Reader on Preaching*, Aldershot: Ashgate, pp. 11–16, p. 15.

21 Long, *The Distance*, p. 15.

22 G. Wingren, 2004, *Luther on Vocation*, Eugene, OR: Wipf and Stock.

23 Barbara Brown Taylor, 2009, *An Altar in the World: Finding the Sacred Beneath our Feet*, Kindle Edition, Norwich: Canterbury Press, Location 196.

24 Taken from https://anglicancommunion.org, accessed 6.3.21.

3

Present to Ourselves

LIZ SHERCLIFF AND MATT ALLEN

Most people have a teacher they remember fondly from their school days. At secondary school, I (Matt) had a form tutor who made an impression on me in my formative years. Although she specialized in foreign languages, she had a broad range of interests. She was warm, witty and well-skilled in managing a classroom of teenagers who had a tendency towards mischief. I recall her simple yet brilliantly effective approach to discipline. She had two questions which she used to keep order in her classes. Her first question would be fired in the direction of general silliness and disruption. She would ask: 'What do you think you are doing?' Most of the time, this was all that was required – the miscreant would stop in their tracks. Her second question was used far more sparingly. No one could mistake the seriousness of their situation when she looked you in the eye and asked: 'Who do you think you are?'

When I think about how we might be present to ourselves as preachers, what comes to mind are the ways those two questions apply to the way we go about preparing to preach. In this first part of this chapter, I will take a look at the first of these questions. Sharing honestly from my experience, I highlight a few things that I have learned about myself which I hope will resonate with other preachers. In the second part of this chapter, Liz will explore aspects of the second question. She will consider these questions: Who do we think we are when we come to read the Bible, and prepare our sermon? and Who do we think we are when we stand to speak? We will finish the chapter by hearing from Saju Muthalaly, a parish priest based in Gillingham, Kent. Saju has also been thinking about who he is as a preacher, especially the importance of his Indian cultural heritage.

What do you think you are doing?

I (Matt) love James's epistle – it is provocative and edgy, and it asks irritatingly incisive questions. Despite some of Martin Luther's famed misgivings, James is of course not proposing a different gospel to Paul, rather his is a crucial voice within the general New Testament witness that reminds us that the ultimate revelation of God's truth is not a message or an idea but the enfleshed, embodied person of Jesus Christ. It is all about Jesus. In Christ, God shows up, so that we be found in him. But we are shown up when we don't let that show. In his epistle, James writes:

> What good is it, my brothers and sisters, if you say you have faith but do not have works? Can faith save you? If a brother or sister is naked and lacks daily food, and one of you says to them, 'Go in peace; keep warm and eat your fill', and yet you do not supply their bodily needs, what is the good of that? So faith by itself, if it has no works, is dead. But someone will say, 'You have faith and I have works.' Show me your faith apart from your works, and I by my works will show you my faith.
> (James 2.14–18)

James gives us a helpful prod when faith is getting lost in heads more than it is being found in our lives. We know that our embodied personal expressions of faith are important. It is not just about what we believe, or say we believe, it matters what we do. We also know that those things are intrinsically linked. That is why it is important to take time to scrutinize what we do in our practice as preachers – our practice is theological just as our theology is practical.

I briefly mentioned in Chapter 1 that several years ago I completed some training in copywriting. I studied for a diploma in this area purely out of personal interest. At the time, I was leading a church in Lancashire and I had a growing sense that I must do something to keep in touch with the reality of people's working lives in commerce and industry. The diploma gave me that opportunity. One of the highlights of that year was spending a couple of weeks of my annual leave temping as a copywriting student at a creative agency near Manchester. It was an integrated agency that delivered live events, digital comms and various forms of marketing and design. There, my eyes were opened to the dramatic pace and high standards of this highly skilled team of illustrators, writers and communications professionals. Driven by the demands of their clients and a commitment to excellence, they would clarify the brief and work instinctively to deliver on what they had agreed. I enjoyed contributing to this team for a couple of weeks. Inevitably, my temporary colleagues took an interest in my regular day job. They wanted to understand how being 'a vicar' overlapped with being a copywriter and the work they did in the agency. As it turned out, there were more similarities than we realized. We talked about writing tributes for funerals and running community events. When it came to discussing the task of week-by-week preaching they were intrigued at the apparent lack of a brief. I described it as 'explaining the Bible' and pointed out that the readings were different each time. Still, one colleague wasn't satisfied and responded: 'Okay, but how do you actually decide what to say in a sermon?' It was a profoundly challenging yet helpful question. They were putting it tactfully, but they were really asking the same question as my teacher: 'What do you think you are doing?'

In my experience, it is remarkably easy to progress along a journey as a preacher without ever stopping to really consider what we think we are doing. In recent years, I have asked every student in one of my preaching classes to explore their aims as preachers by reading the chapter titled 'Why Preach?' from David Heywood's *Transforming Preaching*. I then invite them to complete the exercise below in conversation with other preachers and journal their findings.

What would you say were your aims as a preacher? Consider the following possibilities, add any others you wish and then rank them in order of priority:

- To help people to understand the Bible better.
- To help people to understand and relate to Christian tradition.
- To preach so as to enhance the worship.
- To provoke an encounter with God.
- To challenge people to live distinctive Christian lives.
- To help people to cope with the problems they encounter in their daily lives.
- To lead people to conversion to Christian faith.
- To promote deeper and more authentic relationships among the congregation.
- Others ... [1]

I was surprised how many of the students who have done this report back that the preachers they had spoken to struggled to identify their aims. Based on the students whom I have taught, it seems many preachers model what they do based on what they liked or valued as hearers. I am sure that we can learn a lot this way. We can develop an implicit understanding of the purpose of preaching and find ways of improving at various aspects of that task. Digging a little deeper into what we actually do requires self-awareness and reflexivity. It is about seeing yourself seeing yourself. Back to my colleague in the creative agency, it is about asking at a more personal level: how do I really decide what to say now? What do I think *I* am doing?

What do I think I am doing?

My aims in preaching are not static, they adjust according to context and circumstances. Occasionally, like in the creative agency in which I worked, the 'brief' is more clearly defined. For example, preaching at baptisms, weddings, and funerals is not like preaching to the regular congregation on any given Sunday. On the surface, my aims in preaching at these special services would appear to be quite different. The liturgical context requires something distinctive from the preacher. I would be looking to ensure that I use the sermon to speak to those who have gathered to commemorate or celebrate. Getting to grips with my regular preaching has been trickier, but one common thread has become evident over time. I have identified that I seek to provoke or facilitate an encounter with God. Put in simplistic terms, my understanding of an encounter is something which touches the heart – the inner being which, as Liz explored in Chapter 2, motivates thoughts and actions. I want people to have some kind of inner experience of God's presence or revelation. This is a lofty aim and also one which requires careful scrutiny as it is susceptible to abuse.[2] Growing awareness of the dangers of spiritual abuse means that it is all the more important that preachers hold their motives and aims up to scrutiny and are accountable for how they minister. This is an area where being present and transparent (in the positive sense mentioned in Chapter 1) is a virtue. So, what do I mean about preaching as an encounter with God?

As a university student, I was in a Bible study group with some Christians who seemed keen to label themselves as 'Calvinists'. I didn't know what a Calvinist was at the time, but after a quick internet search I had a vague idea where they were coming from. We didn't always agree, but I admired how these new friends talked about the importance of the heart when it came to faith. Having spent my teenage years in a charismatic evangelical church, it was familiar to think about engaging the emotions when it came to experiences of God. I was aware that faith which rested solely on my feelings was built on very shaky ground, yet the 'heart' felt like an important place of encounter. My university friends seemed to be holding two things in tension: they had a healthy suspicion about their hearts – they talked about an acute awareness of their own sinfulness – still, they saw their hearts as a vital place for God's activity. John Calvin spoke of every sermon being preached by two ministers: one who externally brings God's word to the ear and the other, the Holy Spirit, who internally ministers God's word to the heart.[3] My understanding of Calvinism is that attending to the heart is critical – it is the place where God works to transform the lives of believers. Crucially, this must be a God-centred, not a self-centred exercise.[4] The heart is important, but the hallmarks of what should be trusted are that which begins and ends in God.

What I do to prepare sermons seems fairly unremarkable. Like most preachers, my sermon preparation begins by prayerfully reading the biblical text(s). I do this without commentaries and sometimes in at least a couple of different translations. I am no Hebrew or Greek scholar, but I know enough about biblical translation to ask some relevant questions of the text and so I may look up a few key words or phrases using an interlinear Bible tool online to help me to explore the choices made by translators.[5] I usually copy the text of the passage (from the version which will be read in the service) into a document on my computer and might make a couple of quick notes about the things which stood out at first reading. From here, I will live with the passage for a while. I won't rush to consult commentaries or any other secondary sources – these come later. I will be wrestling with ideas and themes and trying to see what touches my heart before bringing them together into something coherent. I have tried to attend to this element of wrestling in my preparation to work out what I think I am doing.

I wonder in what ways in the past you have felt that God might be trying to tell you something. As I was preparing for ordination as a deacon, right at the end of my training at Cranmer Hall, I attended a Leavers' Retreat at Shepherds Dene. The main speaker was Judy Hirst and the topic was holiness. I remember the stirring talks Judy gave, I made copious notes and felt I learned a lot. In the service at the end of the retreat, as part of the closing worship, Judy anointed our hands with oil. There was a tangible sense of God's presence in that chapel. I left the retreat convinced that I had grown through the experience. Just over a year later, I turned up to Rydal Hall to my ordination retreat (for my ordination as a priest) to discover that the speaker was Judy Hirst and the topic was holiness. Judy and I joked as the retreat began that the content would be familiar to me already. It didn't take long for me to realize that I had done nothing about the things that had spoken to me or the notes I had taken on the previous occasion. God had provided a chance for me to resit the retreat and this time I was going to put it into action.

The standout session for me was the one spent looking at desire, and the reality that, despite the sentiments we might express as we read Psalm 42, our desire is not for God. This is covered in one of the chapters of Judy's *Struggling to be Holy*. We can be hesitant to speak of desire because of its connotations with sex and a sense of privacy. Nonetheless, we need to find appropriate ways to honestly attend to our desires because they are powerful and can call us beyond ourselves; indeed, God speaks to us at that level as the true object and fulfillment of our desire.[6] I remember Judy challenging us directly both times to uncover our desires by writing some sentences beginning 'I want …' and recording the results.

I don't think we grow as preachers until we allow ourselves to be honest about what we really want to do as preachers. I like exercises like the one from Heywood's book earlier. There is real value in exploring our aims. However, it seems to me that talking about aims without attending to our desires will mean that we only explore a tidied up and sanitized version of what is really going on when we prepare to preach. Our aims alone are more likely to be publicly acceptable and flattering to us. Let me be entirely honest here, I agonize over most of my sermons. I'd like to say that I am like Jacob wrestling with God, but I spend far too much time tripping over my own feet before I even begin to grapple! Some years ago, I began to keep a preaching journal to identify what am I trying to do. I made this painfully honest list where I attended to my desire as well as my aims:

Things 'I want' to do as a preacher:

- Engage responsibly yet creatively with scripture.
- Be seen as knowledgeable about the Bible.
- Avoid revealing too much about myself.
- Avoid cliches and tired messages which I feel have been 'overdone'.
- Be credible.
- Be accurate.
- Be memorable.
- Connect with the academy and wider theological insight.
- Take people into the world of the text itself.
- Get people's attention at the beginning, clearly 'contracting' with the congregation.
- Preach sermons I would want to hear.
- Finish well with a crescendo towards a dramatic 'reveal' which draws things together.
- Impress people.
- Have an impact.

What struck me looking at this list was how many of these expectations relied on my own judgement and perception. It surprised me that it was less about what I wanted people to take away from the talk and more about how I want to feel about myself as a preacher. In truth, it is a very mixed list and one I have had to return to so that I might grow to be more Christlike as a preacher. Augustine's *Confessions* are a great encouragement to any who want to acknowledge and explore their own corrigibility with the aim of discovering hope and redemption. I have found that Augustine's lesser-known *Teaching Christianity* likewise offers comfort to preachers who know that our 'manner of life carries more weight' than the grandeur of our utterances, yet that God's grace in Christ can yet be received even when our motives are not as they ought to be.[7]

While it matters to me that preaching engages the heart, I have observed the murkiness of my own heart. As a preacher, my motives are mixed. They include wanting to make a contribution and to impress people. My feelings in sermon preparation flit between anxiety and excitement, nervousness and eager anticipation. I have tried to explore why I make this so hard for myself. A further excerpt from my journal is below:

> I have noticed that in nearly all my sermon preparation there is a point at which I start to visualize myself delivering that talk to that group of people for that occasion. Positively, this means that I am giving thought to the context, audience and setting. However, it also means that I give attention to how I will feel or how I want to feel when delivering this sermon. Is this necessarily a bad thing? For example, at a funeral I may want to feel compassion for the people gathered there. Perhaps I am working on the assumption that I am not a very good actor. I have to feel something genuinely in order to portray it. My preaching preparation seems to be almost as much about getting myself to a place to *feel* as it is about content. My sermons have to move me. If it doesn't move me then this will show. If it moves me, it is more likely to move other people.

I think I have put my finger on something important. As I noted earlier, I am preaching so that others might encounter God. This must mean that as I prepare, I am open to encountering God myself otherwise I am a hypocrite. Hearers can tell if a person is affected by what they are saying. I do not want to be a religious professional, like a chef who prepares food for others. As a preacher, I am putting together a family meal in which I share the experience of dining. It is a meal prepared for now. I am to be present and not excuse myself from joining in. Just as the clay jars contain the real treasure, it is about what God provides through the one who shows up. Grace is never prayed to the one who prepares the food but to the one who gives food.

Asking, 'What do I think I am doing?' and being present to myself as a preacher has led me back round to considering the content of my preaching. In my journalling, I began to realize what it usually took for a sermon to 'sit' right with me and give me assurance that I could preach it with integrity is that I had found a way of putting it together so that it expressed my personal convictions in a way that pointed beyond myself. This is why I have found the words of 2 Corinthians to be so helpful: 'as of God, before God in Christ we speak' (2 Cor. 2.17, Wycliffe Bible). Many times, I have used those words as a filter for what I planned to say. I ask myself 'Am I able to say this with integrity in Christ? Does it ultimately acknowledge who I am in Christ?' If the answer is no, the sermon needs changing. This has been so useful in encouraging me to rein in my aims and desires and submit these to Christ.

Despite the myriad ways I have written and delivered talks on biblical texts, they aren't as varied or expansive as I would like to believe. I remember my delight at seeing and creating word clouds when they were first popular. They are a great tool for analysing the frequency of words in a body of text, giving you a sense of what it is about. In a word cloud, the size of each word in the cloud represents the number of times it occurs in the text. The focus on Jesus in John's Gospel's is unmissable when you see it as a word cloud – there are lots of resources available which have analysed the Bible this way.[8] If our sermons have a common core, we should be able to spot this by looking at what we find ourselves saying over time, the big words and phrases in our preaching.

I think that when we boil it down, most preachers can identify the common cores to their preaching. I can think of preachers whose every sermon seemed to point to the need for forgiveness, others who would find a way to link each talk to their understanding of the atonement, and others still who seemed keen to stress in as many ways as possible the rather unhelpful idea that 'God is kind of nice and pretty normal really'. I wonder if they were aware of how obvious this was to those who had sat under their preaching for a length of time. When I left my most recent parish post to move into a full-time role in training, I stood in front of my congregation and told them something which I am sure they had already worked out years before. (Graciously, they did not tell me so.) I told them that all of my preaching really boiled down to these two core messages:

1 God is always bigger than we think.
2 It is all about Jesus.

One or both of these messages were present in nearly all my sermons and if they don't remember anything else that I preached, they might want to hold on to these. These are not original statements or ideas, and I probably never preached those ideas explicitly as the message of a talk, but I know that all of my preaching orbits around these core convictions.

The second of my core convictions is particularly key. I am walking a well-trodden path here. I immediately hear Paul's words in 1 Corinthians 2.2 where he 'decided to know nothing ... except Jesus Christ, and him crucified'. As a curate I remember my mentor, Andrew Knowles, patiently listening to my inner angst as a preacher before passing on his wisdom in two words: 'preach Jesus'. I note that he was not saying 'preach about Jesus', although this is certainly a good and appropriate thing to do. Timothy Keller's *Preaching: Communicating Faith in an Age of Scepticism* is a great example of a practical book which informs preachers how to read and preach the Bible Christologically. As we preach, it is good if we can help people to see Jesus in this text. But it is even better if we also encounter Jesus in this place and know his presence in all aspects of our lives.

As I have reflected on my core convictions as a preacher, I have realized that whatever I think I am doing, it is only worthwhile if it is part of what of what God is doing.

God's activity and self-revelation is the wider context for anything I do. I am not the primary actor. All of my preaching ought to participate in God's activity as it is in 'the mission of God ... that we find the answer to the question, "Why preach?"'.[9] Preaching belongs within the theology of the *Missio Dei* – it is a 'joining in' with the mission of God. God's activity and revelation is current, working beyond our limits and boundaries. Being present to ourselves should always lead us beyond ourselves because God is always bigger than we think. We only speak because God is speaking. Jesus is how God speaks and Jesus is what God has spoken, it is all about Jesus.[10]

Who do you think you are?

I (Liz) first became aware of my whiteness in the early noughties. I was visiting Mombasa, Kenya. Two things happened. We went into the spice market, and we visited the port. The spice market was bustling and colourful, filled with luminescent yellow and orange spices, and the sparkling smiles of black Africans. Our guide had taken us there because it was not a usual tourist haunt, and so we had the only white faces in evidence. It felt like a magical moment, and my husband decided to take a photograph. Immediately smiles disappeared and hands were stretched out, asking for money. I felt uncomfortable, misjudged even.

Next our guide took us to the port. He stood us by a wooden gate in the wall. Had it not been closed and locked, I could have fitted through it, though its height might have made me instinctively duck. 'I'll take a photograph of you both,' our Kenyan guide said, and he did. 'Thousands of Africans passed through this gate,' he then said. 'Africans who were being traded as slaves. They were beaten, squeezed into the holds of boats, and taken to countries they didn't want to go to. By white people.' Now I knew that I was white, from a colonialist nation that had oppressed and abused the people around me.

I first became aware of my femaleness at university. In my second year I had been secretary of the Christian Union. I spent my third year in France and Germany gaining a fluency in those languages I have long since lost. When I returned the CU was not as I had left it. My replacement as secretary had not maintained the links with good speakers that I had established, and some weeks there had been no speaker at all. I was asked to help out. But before doing so, one of the leaders felt it incumbent upon them to explain that although I was a good secretary, I could not contemplate being 'more' than that. Although there was also a vacancy for president, that was a man's job, women did not lead. Surprisingly, I did not feel angry at the person instructing me, but I did feel resentful at God.

Of course, before either of those two incidents, I *knew* that

I was a white woman. The incidents helped me to understand what that meant.

I begin this part of the chapter with those stories, because they have helped to shape who I am as I write. They also illustrate the issue I want to discuss first, that who we are influences how we read and how we preach, because it is as ourselves that we are present to God.

'Poor little talkative Christianity'

Entering the Marabar Caves in E. M. Forster's *A Passage to India*, Mrs Moore and her companion Adela each come to life-changing realizations. In these dome-like, pitch-black caves all sounds are returned as an identical echo. 'The echo', writes Forster, 'is entirely devoid of distinction. Whatever is said, the same monotonous noise replies … "boum" – utterly dull. Hope, politeness, the blowing of a nose, the squeal of a boot, all produce "boum".' Mrs Moore realizes that all Christianity's words amount to nothing more than that dull uniform sound, and she says: 'poor little talkative Christianity'.

Agree or disagree with the sentiment, it is hard to deny that Christianity can be talkative, and that the more talkative it is the poorer and smaller it becomes.

Being present to God is not 'talkative Christianity', in fact it could well be silent Christianity. Rudolph Bultmann insisted, there can be no such thing as presuppositionless exegesis, meaning that we bring to every text our own pre-conceived ideas. I also believe that our life experience and circumstances affect our reading in ways we need to be aware of. They do so because they position us in relation to a text, thus opening up a particular vista and obscuring others. I do not think that this is a bad thing, I only want to say that it is something we should be aware of. I will return to this point later. For now, let's look at an example of what I mean.

Being 'hemmed in'

During my curacy, my supervising minister decided we would do a preaching series on Psalms. Psalm 139 fell to me. It's a lovely, reassuring psalm about how we were formed by God even from our mother's womb. Or is it? I wondered how those who were ill-formed in their mothers' womb felt about God in light of verse 14 ('I praise you, for I am fearfully and wonderfully made. Wonderful are your works'). Aware of how my faith has been changed by life's experiences, I wondered why the psalmist makes no provision for ongoing formation in verse 13 ('For it was you who formed my inward parts'). My presupposition was that this was a psalm of comfort. Recognizing that this was my idea, and not necessarily what the psalm says for everyone encouraged me to read further. As a preacher who believes in living a preaching life rather than preparing sermons, I would have loved verse 14 to read: 'I am being fearfully and wonderfully made.' It doesn't. It might – the Hebrew is 'a mess' as the expert I consulted put it – but the link is too tenuous to do anything more than suggest. Robert Alter (who is substantially more reliable than my wishful thinking!) translates verse 14 like this: 'I acclaim you, for fearsomely I am set apart.'[11] At least that translation links with Pauline ideas of being set apart for the Gospel (Romans 1.1) or the Church as the body of Christ. Sometimes it is the title given to biblical passages in particular translations that should give pause for thought. The NRSV entitles Psalm 139 *The Inescapable God*. Why and whom might someone want to escape? The words are shot through with inescapability – 'You know when I sit down and when I rise up', 'You hem me in, behind and before, and lay your hand upon me', 'Where can I go from your spirit?' – what is heard is 'Where can I go from you?' For abused, oppressed or controlled people these words seem far from reassuring. This psalm, then, does not say something I would like it to say, and does say things I would like it not to say. Working with it was far more challenging that I had anticipated. It provided a good reminder that as a preacher I am hemmed in, not by God but by my ability to see beyond my own perspective.

Theology in a clay jar

I often ask, at the start of a course on preaching, what students think preaching is and what the role of the preacher might be. Almost every time I have asked that question at least one person has said that the preacher should be invisible – something like the glass jar, explored in Chapter One, that we can look through to see the sparkling contents. Sometimes would-be preachers quote John the Baptist's line 'He must increase, but I must decrease' (John 3.30). 'I don't want to be seen,' the students tell me, 'I want people to see Jesus.' Such sentiments sound admirable – at first. But, in the end, they are misguided. We need to be in it to point to Jesus. The first thing that happens when we stand to speak is that we are seen. That is particularly true if in some way we diverge from the traditional expectation of a white, well-educated, able-bodied male. A Professor of Sociology and writer, Michael Kimmel, says:

> To be white, or straight, or male, or middle class is to be simultaneously ubiquitous and invisible. You're everywhere you look, you're the standard against which everyone else is measured. You're like water, like air. People will tell you they went to see a 'woman doctor' or they will say they went to see 'the doctor'. People will tell you they have a 'gay colleague' or they'll tell you about a colleague. A white person will be happy to tell you about a 'Black friend', but when that same person simply mentions a 'friend', everyone will assume the person is white. Any college course that doesn't have the word 'woman' or 'gay' or 'minority' in its title is a course about men, heterosexuals and white people. But we call those courses 'literature', 'history' or 'political science'.[12]

The same is true of sermons – they are delivered either by a preacher, or by a woman/black/disabled/gay preacher. The idea of not being visible simply does not work for many of us when the first thing the congregation does is to see us. Preachers are not invisible jars holding God's word for the congregation, from which God's instruction will flow unadulterated. Rather we are clay jars, like those we have already mentioned. Clay jars can hold the same refreshing water, they pour it out in the same way as glass jugs, but clay jars are seen. Back to what I wish Psalm 139.14 said! God continues to shape us in ways that can make our sermons distinctive, as well as beautiful, if only we are present to the possibilities.

Masks, hiding and protecting

'Rather like politicians or celebrities we develop an image of ourselves that is our shop window, the person we want others to think we are (and increasingly the person we want to see ourselves as' I (Liz) wrote in my earlier book *Preaching Women* (2019). I talked about wearing masks as an aide to promoting the desired image of ourselves. At the time the link was with Jungian psychology. Since then, thanks to the Covid-19 pandemic, masks have become associated with something quite different – as I write we are at a stage in history when 'have you got a mask?' seems to be a common question on leaving the house. We can, then, hide behind masks – project the confident courageous preacher, even though the real person is uncertain and a bit afraid. Preachers' fears are varied, often rooted in the nitty gritty of everyday life. What happens if I don't attract new people? What if I preach what that passage seems to say and upset the congregation? What if they can hear the doubt in my voice?

Let's think about some masks a preacher might be tempted to use:

- *The Pantomime Mask*
  This mask exists to help audiences suspend reality and enter into the pantomime moment. We are swept along by the presence on stage, and the reactions of the crowd, shouting 'it's behind you' or booing when the 'villain' enters the stage. People often like church this way, and go there to escape the problems of the world. As preachers we collude with this mindset whenever we choose to be overprotective, to

keep the congregation happy, or to avoid difficult questions. I recently spent some time with a group of students exploring the Parable of the Talents. We did some exegetical work, read some commentaries and decided that the 'talents' in question could only mean money, and could have nothing to do with gifts or skills, at least for Jesus' original hearers.[13] 'So,' I asked the group, 'would you preach that?' Nobody said they would.

- *The Gangster Mask*
  Gangster masks symbolize power – a power that only exists because people believe it does. It is manipulative and utterly committed to particular interests, power resides in the ability to shut down discussion and enforce consent. As a teenager I once managed to take a family member to church for the first time. I felt quite pleased with myself. The preacher was one of the church elders. Always a 'shouter', on this occasion he outdid himself with threats about hell fire and damnation, and his confidence that his gospel was correct. For the first time, I heard his words through the ears of an outsider, and was horrified. The 'gangster' attitude seeks to get people onboard, insists on loyalty, and determines whose voice will be heard and whose will not.

- *The Beautician Mask*
  Beautician masks have one basic purpose, to minimize or hide blemishes and enhance what is good. Preachers might use beauticians' masks to wilfully forget their church's past, or to disown its story. The Living in Love and Faith discussion in the Church of England has generated many comments revelatory of this kind of technique: 'they are liberal/conservative, they would say that wouldn't they?' In other areas of faith, Celtic Christianity looks more attractive when conversion by warfare is airbrushed out, Christian mission looks more worthy when decoupled from its imperialist exploitation, and Wesley looks inspirational if we ignore his neglect of his wife. Likewise the Psalms are a source of comfort when we overlook the writers' desires for God to slay

their enemies, and David is a great king as long as we ignore his treatment of almost every woman he had dealings with.

- *The Virus Mask*
  One of the most difficult messages to get across during the recent pandemic seems to have been that wearing a mask protected others from you, rather than the other way round. Sometimes the congregation might need their preacher to wear just such a mask, one that will prevent them spreading banality, propaganda and lies.

Preaching is not about hunting down and spearing the truth of a text in order to present it, fresh-cooked, to a hungry congregation. Rather it is about openness – being present to God and to the congregation. Being present to the congregation is the stuff of a later chapter; here, having laid some foundations, I want to focus on being present to God.[14]

- *The Venetian Mask*
  Fans of period drama will be familiar with the Venetian, or masquerade, mask. It is part of costume, usually for a high society ball. The purpose of the mask is to complete the costume. It is not held permanently over the face, and is usually lowered once the user has found a suitable conversation partner. This mask illustrates the use of commentaries in sermon preparation and delivery. They might complement our outfit, for a while they might come between us and our hearers, but for real communication to take place, they must be lowered, so that our conversation partners can see the real us.

Have the courage to show up and be seen

In her inspiring book *Daring Greatly*, Brené Brown speaks of praying 'give me the courage to show up and let myself be seen'. I can't think of a better prayer for a preacher, either when we come before God and to the text, or when we stand before the congregation. Being seen is a biblical idea. God searches and knows us (Psalm 139), Jesus knows his sheep (John 10.14–15). Praying before we begin to read or write can sometimes be little more than a tick-box exercise. It can also lull us into a false sense of security, allowing us to believe that whatever we choose to say from that point on is God's word for the congregation, something from which our hearers should be protected. Showing up and being seen is more challenging and goes deeper. It is why I believe that those of us called to preach should think not about preparing sermons, but about living a preaching life.

My body, my voice

'Preaching is personal communication, and it can only be done in our own bodies, in our own voices.'[15] To be authentically ourselves we need first of all to know who we are in God's presence. I don't mean by constructing the kind of identikit image of ourselves assembled in some Christian posters from various biblical promises. I mean who I am and who you are that makes us unique. Who have we been, who are we, who are we becoming?

Nobody else could tell that story, it has shaped only me. It is part of my past and part of my present, it shapes what goes on within me and it shapes what comes out of me. One aspect of my story as told above means that whenever I read 1 Corinthians 11.27–32 I interpret the 'unworthy manner' of taking communion, the failure to discern the body, as failing to realize that all are welcome at the Lord's table. It affects my choice of pre-communion prayer too. Given a choice, I am likely to be inclusive, saying something like 'come to this table not because you are strong, but because you are weak ... because you love the Lord a little and would like to love him more'.

Being present to God means being present to ourselves. If we take seriously the critique of Psalm 139, above, we cannot believe that God forces us to be known. I believe that there must be an element of openness to God first. As preachers that means understanding why we think what we think, why we interpret the Bible in the ways that we do, and being open to conversation with God. Truth in the context of being present to God is openness, or hospitality. God is constantly open to being in relationship with us, and it is through this relationship that we are formed as preachers with beautiful truths to share.

My body and my voice are unique. They each have attributes that make them so. These attributes impact my reading of the Bible, my understanding of the world and my faith in God. Let's think about what these attributes might be and how they might steer my Bible reading.

Location

During the second Covid lockdown beers were brewed, T-shirts and sweatshirts printed and songs sung proclaiming the then Mayor of Greater Manchester, Andy Burnham, as King of the North. Greater Manchester had been in lockdown for four months, its economy was being decimated and the Westminster government seemed not to care. People gathered around a local hero. Bodies come from certain areas which impart certain identities and create community in the face of perceived adversity. In my Bible reading during that time, I'm sure my sensitivity to the marginalized was heightened. Reading Mary's song in Luke 1.46–55 in preparation for an Advent sermon I was very aware of the promise that God scatters the proud and brings down the powerful. Where we are from geographically can contribute to how our bodies and how our voices sound, which can lead to unacknowledged prejudices in those who see and hear us. Being aware of ourselves, and acknowledging our own backgrounds, enables us to speak from that place, and allow for our congregation to be different.

Marital status might affect our preaching – do we praise marriage and avoid speaking of singleness? If we are very pro-marriage, do we avoid the difficulties presented by stories in the Old Testament? Does our Bible-reading assume that children are a blessing from God? That might lead to the common trope that David was right to get up and get on after his child died (2 Samuel 12.15–23), but it leaves women who have suffered miscarriage or early child death without comfort.

Political commitments and theological positions likewise affect our Bible reading. The risk here is that they can lead us to sound as though ours is the only way of reading particular passages. Luke 4.16–30 provides two useful examples.

Teaching the Gospel according to Luke as part of a pre-ordination course I asked students to storyboard the events, first without referring to the text and then with the text in front of them. The storyboard without benefit of the text went something like this:

> Jesus goes to the synagogue – he reads from the prophet Isaiah – he tells the people that he is the one who fulfilled the Scriptures – the people get angry and decide to get rid of him.

Reading the text of Luke, of course, this is not what happens at all. After Jesus handed back the scroll and said: '"Today this scripture has been fulfilled in your hearing." All spoke well of him and were amazed at the gracious words that came from his mouth' (4.22). It was when Jesus began to say that other nations counted among God's people that they wanted to throw him off a cliff. Having established that that was what the Bible says, one student said: 'I still prefer the other version, so that's what I will preach.'

The second example comes from a conference, where I was speaking about Jesus' inclusive gospel. I had begun to read this passage from Luke 4 when one young man shouted out: 'I know what you are going to say, and I disagree'. The power of our predetermined theological positions not only prevents us from hearing other perspectives, but causes us to hold on to our own so tightly that we believe it to be absolute truth.

Life stage

Perhaps it is our life stage that most clearly influences how we preach. Certainly, when I look back over 30 plus years of preaching, I notice how what I say has changed. Probably until March 2020, I would have preached about the Body of Christ gathering together, perhaps encouraging everyone to make room for communal worship in their week. Now we have to consider that staying away from worship might be for the good of everyone. Until the political disputes that arose out of Brexit, it was not really necessary in sermons to think about what it means to be part of a particular nation, in fact themes of rebuilding walls from Nehemiah were often chosen by churches seeking to be missional. Life stage is not just personal, it is communal, national and global too.

One of my tasks as a preacher is to hold up the gospel so that others can see it clearly from where they are. It is not to get others to see it from where I am. To do that, I need to be clear about where I am and what other perspectives are possible.

Who do you think you are? Saju's story

I am thinking about who I am at a key moment. Being born in India, I have now lived half my life in the East and nearly half my life in the West. That it is half-and-half feels like a unique privilege because not many people have that kind of symmetry to where they have lived. I look back at myself as a 20 year-old and the actual excitement I felt as I (and I use the word carefully) incarnated myself in a new context. Moving to England and living in the West was the 'big thing' for me as a young Indian man. I arrived here, thinking 'wow, what might be the possibilities for me in a gap year?' Twenty years later, I am still here. That potential has turned into a reality that has been more than I could have imagined. Yet, at the very same time, there is also a loss. There is a loss of connections. There is a loss in the last 20 years of the homeland. There's a loss, in some ways, of relationships, because the friends I grew up with, and my cousins and family, are scattered all over the world. There is the loss of language. English is my second language, but I now have to think hard of very common terms in my mother tongue. This loss of language has meant a loss of stories and a loss of memories.

What I have only just realized is that what I have been doing in the last 20 years is trying to replace what was going on before. Becoming myself in this land has been partly shaped by me attempting to tell the church here, 'Hey listen, I might look Indian. I might sound Indian, but actually, I can cut it here. I can make sense here.' Therefore, I have been overcompensating and editing myself in many ways by actually saying, 'Listen, I'm not going to talk about my Indian background any more because I don't want you to think that actually, this Indian guy can't cut it in the church in the West.' In replacing that original cultural heritage I have found and enjoyed being part of a new one in England. One of the things the Lord has been challenging me on recently is that this is one of those things which is a 'both/and', not an 'either/or'.

It is an issue, for example, that in my preaching all my original cultural references and illustrations have been almost exclusively Westernized. What I have recently noticed is that no one has ever asked me why. When I do talk about my Indian cultural heritage, in fact nearly every time I've done it in my preaching, I am hearing from the congregation: 'We want you to do that some more because we don't get that from other preachers: we want more of that.' This has been a revelation. I am waking up to a realization where I am starting to say 'Ah, maybe I don't need to hide it. Maybe I don't need to kill it. Maybe I don't need to replace it. Maybe I just need to attend to it.' For 20 years I have assumed that people are not interested in Indian stories, Indian backgrounds and Indian ways of thinking; actually, the opposite is true.

Now I am finding myself relearning my heritage. As I had been forgetting the Malayalam liturgy, which was so formative, I asked my uncle to send me recordings of his prayers so I can listen to them on my walks and runs. There's something about hearing people praying in my mother tongue – it has been so moving. We know that you don't have to speak Hebrew or Greek or English or Latin to connect with God. As I connect with God in my mother tongue I get a sense of how God has made everything beautiful. God has made it possible for all languages to be redeemed and so praying in my mother tongue again has been very important to me.

The other thing is I have rediscovered is that the Bible is more of an Eastern book than it is an English book. For years I have enjoyed the work of Kenneth Bailey who makes this point: The Bible is far more an Eastern book than a Western book. If you read this as a Western book, you are very likely to misunderstand it on a regular basis. Rediscovering my cultural heritage has helped me to see the value of positive forms of argument, similar to those within the Jewish tradition, which are valuable to me as a preacher. I am seeing in the biblical text elements of what has been called Indian argumentativeness, something explored by Amartya Sen in a well-known book called *Argumentative Indian*. It is not about disagreement but rather a reminder that I am naturally inclined to read the text with others. I have noticed how going into the study to prepare a sermon on my own is at odds with this and completely different to the communal way we would attend to a text in India where there would be collaborative collective thinking around any divine or human issues. I have always felt alone in the task of preaching and I am now seeing why that is.

If I want to be true to my cultural heritage in my preaching, then I feel I need to learn how to be a hospitable preacher. India is a hospitable culture, despite the Hindutva movement which is hostile towards Muslims, Christians and minorities. Historically, it's been a culture that embraced everything including any worldviews. So, 'Jesus? Oh yes, we'll include him as well. An imperial power from Persia? Yes, we'll include them as well. The British? Yes, we'll include that. Dutch? Yes.' It is a culture that soaks in. *The Indian culture is comfortable in its heritage to adopt other worldviews.* I think this is because deep down the people are very hospitable. Hospitality isn't acceptance of every idea, but it does mean a welcome for every person. As a hospitable preacher, I ought to create a space where people can taste the gospel in an Indian cup or an English cup or a Dutch cup. The preaching I seek to nurture would then engender a warm place. A place where learning happens. A place of laughter. A place of tears. But a lot of the time that hasn't been my experience. Preaching has been colder, it has been distant.

The question was: 'Who do you think you are as a preacher?' My answer to that is: 'Someone who takes their shoes off.' I say this because this is literally what I do when I preach. I take my shoes off to remind myself that preaching is a holy task. I take my shoes off because I am encountering God and I want you to encounter God. It is an indicator of my desire to be fully myself and honour my cultural heritage. If you go to a Hindu temple in India, or if you go to an Orthodox church or Catholic church, or even an Anglican church in India, the first thing you do is take your shoes off. You leave the shoes outside the church building, the temple and the home. In some Indian contexts it is very rude to walk into someone's house with your shoes on. Taking my shoes off is a gesture that is intended to express humility and vulnerability among others. From there I offer what I have to bring.

I do think I have something distinctive to bring as myself. I'm increasingly thinking that we are very quick to highlight the poetry of people like George Herbert or even Shakespeare, yet I have, not in the church in India, nor in a church in England, ever heard anyone mention Rabindranath Tagore or Sarojini Naidu. These are outstanding poets. I want to be able to say, 'Why?' There is in my mind a form of intellectual cultural colonialism that goes on, which actually says some voices are acceptable in a sermon and some voices are not. Digging deep inside, it's not necessarily wisdom or depth of insight because, I think, Tagore and Naidu and all kinds of poets in the Global South, bring a lot of insight into our human condition and the activity of God. Even though I haven't in the past, I can mention those in the future and take different opportunities to speak from my experience as I open the scriptures with others in my preaching. Maybe I need to demonstrate that my heritage actually matters a lot in my preaching, especially if it means I can preach in places in which it is clear that we live in a globalized society. Maybe my heritage matters because I am meant to preach as me, as I am, within the context of a given community. As a preacher, both my feet may be planted here, but I do not need to pretend that my life does not straddle two continents.

Questions for further reflection

- What are your aims as a preacher? How might also considering your desires change the way you see these?

- Is there a common core to your preaching – a consistent message which is distinctively yours and which you own with conviction?

- Which of the masks described in this chapter are you most likely to wear when preaching?

- Acknowledging that your personality, perspective, and past and present experience are all part of who you are as a preacher and ways in which God has formed you for the role. It is worth taking time to reflect on what kind of preacher you are.

  Here are ten helpful questions to consider:
  1. What do people see when I stand to preach?
  2. Is what they see an advantage or might it be a barrier?
  3. How do I sound to myself and to others?
  4. Is my accent/voice/use of words an advantage or might it be a barrier?
  5. What significant experiences have I had?
  6. What is happening in my life now?
  7. What are the quiet zones in my preaching – what topics do I avoid?
  8. What ideas do my hearers associate with me?
  9. Which masks am I most tempted to hide behind?
  10. What in my preaching shows what I believe about Jesus?

Notes

1 David Heywood, 2013, *Transforming Preaching*, London: SPCK, p. 11.

2 Some timely attention is being given to spiritual abuse. See, for instance Lisa Oakley and Justin Humphreys, 2019, *Escaping the Maze of Spiritual Abuse*, London: SPCK. Also, the work of my colleague Amy White who is currently writing to this working title for Grove Books: *Towards a Spiritual Definition of Spiritual Abuse*.

3 I am paraphrasing Joel Beeke's exploration of this in his 2008 book *Living for God's Glory: An Introduction to Calvinism*, Kindle Edition, Lake Mary, FL: Reformation Trust, Location 2493.

4 Joel Beeke explores the theocentrism of Calvinsim *Living for God's Glory*, Location 1083.

5 The online tool I use most often in looking at biblical languages is the Bible Hub website – https://biblehub.com/interlinear/.

6 This is a summary of 'Dealing with our Desires', in Judy Hirst, 2006, *Struggling to be Holy*, London: Darton, Longman and Todd, pp. 42–52.

7 Augustine draws on scriptures such as Philippians 1.18 to make this point (Augustine, 2014, *Teaching Christianity*: *De Doctrina Christiana*, Kindle Edition, translated by Edmund Hill and John E. Rotelle, Hyde Park: NY, New City Press, Location 9192.)

8 The most comprehensive resource I have found for this is the collection of word clouds on the Blue Letter Bible website – https://www.blueletterbible.org/images/wordclouds/

9 Heywood, *Transforming Preaching*, p. 13.

10 In teaching notes prepared for doctrine students, Tom Woolford puts the same point in similar words: 'In summary, the Son is both the *mode* and the *content* of God's final, definitive revelation. He is *how* God speaks, and he is *what* God says: he is, in the words of the apostle John, the Word made flesh' (Tom Woolford, 2018).

11 R. Alter, 2007, *The Book of Psalms: A Translation with Commentary*, New York: W. W. Norton.

12 M. Kimmel, 2016, *Privilege: A Reader*, New York: Routledge.

13 See for example Amy-Jill Levine, 2015, *Short Stories by Jesus*, New York, HarperCollins.

14 I am indebted to Glen Marshall, Co-Principal of the Northern Baptist College, for the ideas I have developed here. They spring from a paper Glen gave at the 2020 Manchester Preaching Conference.

15 Gay, Doug, 2018, *God be in My Mouth: 40 ways to grow as a preacher*, Edinburgh: St Andrew Press, p. 82.

4

Present to the Bible

LIZ SHERCLIFF AND MATT ALLEN

There's a wonderful cartoon you may have seen that illustrates some approaches to the Bible. The scene is a car showroom. Salespeople stand around shiny motors. In the doorway two people are talking, one says to the other 'I asked what Jesus would buy,' as he leaves the showroom on a donkey. Being present to the Bible means going beyond simplistic, even apparently obvious interpretations. It means preaching not only like Paul, who preached rhetorically, or Moses, who preached prophetically, or Deborah, whose voice celebrated God and her people. It means also preaching like Jacob – wrestling with the text until it has first of all changed us.

Preaching like Jacob

The writer of Genesis is short on detail. All we know of the scene, is that Jacob has sent his possessions and his family ahead of him. Jacob's first aim was appeasement, the avoidance of conflict, and he didn't mind gambling with others' futures to achieve it – he gave his household no better than a fifty-fifty chance, after all. His wives and children are gone too, sent across the river where he hopes they will be safe. There is nothing and no one to protect him. He is alone and 'a man wrestled with him till daybreak' (Genesis 32.24). How does it start? Do Jacob and the man circle round each other, watchful, waiting for someone to make the first move, before they engage? Is Jacob taken by surprise, alone and with no alternative but to fight or die? How do we imagine this epic wrestling

– restrained, more show than fight? Or a fierce, punishing fight to exhaustion? Jacob's damaged hip suggests the latter. However we might explain it theologically, this seems to be a real fight. Wrestling is close fighting. There is no standing back and swinging punches here, this fight is intended to throw Jacob off balance, to make him yield rather than knock him out. But Jacob, surely the weaker partner, demands a blessing, and because he accepts the challenge, enters the fight and refuses to give in, God blesses him.

Suppose we use this fight as a metaphor for preaching. We have the option of appeasing the congregation, of planning a sermon that sends on ahead of the main message some words that allow the congregation to interpret the text as they please. A sentence for literalists here, a word for sceptics there and surely everyone will be appeased. Perhaps rather than wrestle the text, we take a swing at it from historical-critical, doctrinal or traditional perspective, thus keeping it safely at arm's length. But if we do that we will miss out on the encounter and run the risk of avoiding the 'now' in our preaching.

In Jacob's story, wrestling with God has a profound effect. Next day, when he sees Esau approaching, Jacob goes *ahead* of his family. Has the cowardly appeaser been transformed into a confident leader? As he approaches Esau he bows seven times, as a servant would before a master. Although Jacob is in possession of their father's blessing and inheritance, he acknowledges Esau's position. Preaching means acknowledging our own position and that of our hearers, confident that God has been at work in our wrestling and will speak from our experience.

Travelling the road

As practical theologians we believe that the travelling reveals more about personal theology than the intended destination or the arrival. That is, that watching and listening to ourselves and others shows us far more about underlying beliefs than do statements of faith. Many a woman must have said they admired Mary's calm attention to Jesus as she sat at his feet, while all the while wondering how anything ever got done. Many a preacher has probably denied the existence of a sacred–secular divide while speaking as though church work trumps all other activity. The routes we take through our faith can be as constructed as the major routes through our towns and villages, or as off-road as mountain walks. We can choose to stick to the well-defined, or to go off and explore. The real question is whether or not we are willing. In her wonderful book *Learning to Walk in the Dark*, Barbara Brown Taylor speaks of exploring darkness. On one occasion she is invited to go into a 'wild' cave, one that has not been mapped or domesticated for tourism. Inside the cave, reaching to turn off her lamp so that she might surrender to the dark, Taylor notices an 'impossibly sparkly' stone. She puts it into her bag as a souvenir. Once back in her room she takes out the stone – now 'pigeon coloured, with a faint sparkle along one side.' 'What in the world made me think this was a precious stone?' she wonders, before realizing that 'the stone is not the problem. The light is the problem.'[1]

Light can be the problem with preaching too, because light leads us to believe that we know where we are, and where we are going. John of the Cross regarded darkness as God's best gift, intended for our liberation. God puts out our lights to keep us safe, for according to John 'God will enlighten the soul, giving it knowledge ... of the greatness and excellence of God.'[2] When we can no longer see the road ahead, when we can no longer read the map we brought with us, and we can no longer sense anything around us that might guide us through the dark, then and only then do we allow ourselves to rely solely on God.

Sydney Carter's simple song 'One more step along the world I go' has extraordinary reach. Many couples who learned it at school still choose it for their wedding. The final verse, drawing on words of St Augustine, holds profound truth:

> You are older than the world can be,
> You are younger than the life in me;

Ever old and ever new,
Keep me travelling along with you.
And it's from the old I travel to the new;
Keep me travelling along with you.[3]

When we grasp that the one who is 'ever old and ever new' travels alongside us and speaks to us as we engage with the scriptures, the sense of anticipation and excitement that accompany exploration seems to us to be entirely appropriate. Neither closed-minded traditionalism nor amnestic revisionism do justice to the One with whom we journey: ever old *and* ever new. Biblical interpretation, particularly in our post-truth era, has become gang warfare for some. Instead of sticking the boot in, let's stick our boots on and see where the adventure leads us.

Ever old and ever new

For reasons related to church tradition[4] we both ended up speaking about the same reading at different times – Matt in December 2020 and Liz in January 2021. This is Matt's story:

I am sure that all preachers will be able to identify with that feeling when you read what you thought was a familiar text and you discover in it something you had managed to miss completely up to this point. I recently became aware of just how easy it is to read the text you think you know, rather than the actual text in front of you. I consider myself well acquainted with Matthew's Gospel. (I would like to say that this was a result of careful study, but it is probably just as likely to be the result of too many failed attempts in the past to read the New Testament in one sitting.) As is often the case around Christmas and Epiphany, I found myself preparing a talk on Matthew's Magi. In your typical nativity story, we meet the Magi when, on their stargazing trip, they turn up at the palace to see King Herod. That was pretty much what I thought I had read in the text every time I had done so, but that's not quite how it happens and, as it turns out, the Magi aren't quite as informed as I had assumed them to be. The Magi go to *Jerusalem* and they seem to be asking around: 'Where is the one who has been born king of the Jews?'[5] Then, in verse 3 we read: 'When King Herod heard this, he was frightened, and all Jerusalem with him'.

Wherever the Magi had been, it was not behind the closed doors of the palace but more likely out on the streets. We might want to explore why all of Jerusalem was frightened. It is interesting to see what happens when we dig into this further, as I did in the talk I eventually wrote.

Having spotted something I had missed in my prior readings of Matthew 2, I found myself considering the fragile form of peace in which life existed at the time in a nation under Roman occupation. This meant noting the place of Jerusalem politically, given the north–south divide in the country. The sermon I wrote included this brief section:

> Caught up in the life of the city, those in Jerusalem had kept their position in society by proving their utility to Rome. Collect the taxes, maintain civil order and keep your heads down. That will do for them for now. It is at least a toe in the door that leads to the corridors of power. A Messiah would be marvellous, but it will need to be a full-sized solution not a half-baked notion like a special baby. Until something substantial was on offer, anything that upset the status quo and provoked the Romans was a source of fear, not hope. For those clinging onto some form of power and influence, a bunch of strange foreigners making a public scene on the streets of the city and talking about a new-born King of the Jews sounds like serious trouble; it was certainly the stuff of Herod's nightmares. Herod takes some initiative. He summons the religious leaders and asks where the Messiah is to be born. He receives his answer from the scriptures: Bethlehem. Then, in Matt 2.7, Herod *secretly* calls for the Magi. He does not publicly associate with them. He can't! Yet in the interaction which follows, Herod becomes the one who informs the Magi where to find the child – becoming another example of Israel and the scriptures pointing to Jesus.

Somehow previously I had missed a key detail in the text and overlooked so many dimensions to the story. I ought not to be so sure that I know what the Bible says before I read it. I should remember to relish every fresh encounter.

Liz's reading of the text was new not because of a fresh reading of the text, but because of unprecedented world events. On 6 January, Epiphany, 2021 a mob attacked the Capitol building in Washington DC, the capital of the United States. It was, according to many, an attempted coup. Allegedly, the crowd had been incited by the then president, who was about to be replaced. A man afraid of losing power unleashed terrible violence. Parallels are clear!

In Chapter 2, Liz talked about the importance of the inquisitiveness that leads us to find unexpected things in unexpected places. It's how beachcombers discover unusual pebbles or rare shells. The same inquisitiveness, or curiosity, leads us to abandon the well-trodden path in pursuit of adventure.

Curiosity

Recently, over Zoom with some friends, I (Matt) have been engaging with a fantastic new resource for small groups who want to focus on personal growth as disciples of Jesus. 'The Character Course' has been developed by Roger Bretherton, a clinical psychologist and Lecturer at Lincoln University. Its aim is to bring fresh insights from psychology together with the ancient wisdom of the scriptures; it explores themes like hope, love and forgiveness.[6] The final session is on curiosity. Curiosity, it turns out, is linked to wellbeing and happiness and helps us to grow, including spiritually.[7] The script for this session of the course includes a reminder that at the start of John's Gospel, in John 1.38, Jesus asks his disciples: 'What are you looking for?'; it begins a theme that continues throughout John's Gospel.[8] The session goes on to explain that 'seeking' in the New Testament is similar to what we might call curiosity – the Greek word frequently used is *zeteo* which often 'implies searching for something that otherwise would be hidden'.[9] The related Greek word *syzeteo* is also found in the scriptures; it points to inquiry alongside others. Having a sense of curiosity involves being prepared to wrestle, explore and question things with other people while anticipating discovery.[10] It made me wonder how committed we are to really search the scriptures together to find things that might have be hidden.

The density of a text can sometimes obscure things as we read the Bible. Curiosity is vital to ensuring we ask searching questions that plumb its depths. Margaret Cooling talks about the importance of 'unfolding the text'. As readers we pay attention to what is in the text, or implied by the text within its setting, and unfold it. Using our imaginations, we can recreate the sights, smells, sounds and scenery.[11] Cooling offers a stirring example of this from the beginning of Exodus 2:

> Now a man from the house of Levi went and married a Levite woman. The woman conceived and bore a son; and when she saw that he was a fine baby, she hid him three months. When she could hide him no longer she got a papyrus basket for him, and plastered it with bitumen and pitch; she put the child in it and placed it among the reeds on the bank of the river.[12]

It's striking how easily we miss the import of the short 'she hid him for three months'. It must have been an agonizing time in that household, as Cooling points out. Unfolding the text, we come up against the toll of trying to hide a new-born baby boy. The family's fear for his life, their attempts to avoid discovery, their necessary suspicion of their potentially informant neighbours.[13] The family are pushed to breaking point, physically, emotionally and spiritually. Each barely muffled cry a cause for alarm; every visitor greeted with suspicion. Eventually, they can hide the baby no longer and take him to the river. How might Moses' family have felt at this point? How might such reflection grow our understanding and appreciation of the story? What questions might we now look up elsewhere in the text or in commentaries? In this example we are also reminded of the value of exploring with others. Parents who have nursed or fed unsettled infants would have insights to offer any reading of this text. They might also note that the mother hides the child. Was she the one who kept going when everyone else had given up? Are we curious to know more?

Getting stuck in

So far in this chapter we have thought about preaching as wrestling, exploring and being curious. What links them all is 'getting stuck in'. Getting up close to the text, wandering around in it, unafraid of the dark spots or the hidden things; and all of this prompted by the life-giving gift of curiosity. Before we are curious about the biblical text, it will help to think about our attitudes to the Bible. In which direction does our curious gaze fall? For some, investigation involves the pursuit of objective truth. Failing to uncover it will, objectivists say, result in us massaging the Bible into saying whatever we want it to say. Objectivity is paramount. On the other hand, expecting to find objective truth in the Bible, say others, is to force it into a mould it does not fit, a source of sermon material, or life coaching, rather than the story of God and God's people. Both positions restrict the text to what Mikhail Bakhtin describes as 'small time' by enclosing its meaning in either its original setting, or the present, rather than allowing these two to work together dialectically.[14] It seems to us that the last thing we ought to be doing with the Bible is closing it down. We should be doing precisely the opposite – opening it up!

What then, do we want to say about biblical authority? And where is the ground on which we both can stand? We are guided by the thoughts of N. T. Wright, which he has repeated in many lectures, papers and books. Firstly, we acknowledge that God has given us the Bible we need. It is no mistake that it is primarily narrative by nature and ancient in origin.[15] Wright uses the analogy of an unfinished Shakespeare play in the hands of experienced Shakespearean actors. Acts 1–4 are Creation, Fall, Israel and Jesus and the

Church. Act 5 is where we are now. As experienced actors with material to work with, we are able to produce a final act that is as close to what God, the author, intended, as possible.[16] Ever old, ever new, ever now.

Over the past few years, we have taught preaching to groups of final year ordinands at a residential held in Holy Week. Final year ordinands have generally become well-versed in critical study of the Bible. Most will have undertaken several biblical studies modules by the time they come to this preaching class. Some will have moved during training from engaging in almost entirely pre-critical readings of scripture to embrace new approaches. In addition, there will be those whose training for Christian ministry, whose encounter with critical study of the Bible has rocked their faith and obliterated their ability to be immersed in the text.

For some, biblical studies undermines confidence in Bible reading. It fails to ignite the excitement about the scriptures that might sustain them as disciples and ministers in years to come. This was certainly my (Matt) experience of ministerial training. Theological study was hugely disorientating and, at times, counterproductive. Thankfully, I had wise guides and good friends around me who helped me navigate the route back to solid ground. I began to understand how I could return to many familiar patterns of Bible reading. Perhaps, in Paul Ricœur's language, I came to a 'second naïveté'.[17] In truth, I was now equipped with a raft of new questions to bring to the text, but instead of complicating what I was doing in an unhelpful way they reminded me that all human knowing is partial. I mistakenly thought critical study was teaching me how to do it 'right'. I was wrong – it was informing me how to do it better by doing it as myself and thinking about what I was doing.

When faced with a class of final year ordinands, we try to bear in mind how deskilled some of them may be feeling when it comes to reading the Bible as preachers. We are aware of how unclear some of them might be about what they are doing when they come to interpret the Bible. In one of our sessions, which always proves to be a highlight, we ask students to explore a passage of scripture by creating a three-dimensional representation of what they read with dolly pegs to represent the people. We call it the 'dolly peg' exercise. The sight of hundreds of wooden dolly pegs never fails to ignite the imagination. The exercise highlights participatory reading of scripture. It grows our awareness and understanding of what we do when we read the Bible, how we enter the world of the text. It is an immersive experience through which we learn how to grow our knowledge *of* the text.

We begin the exercise by looking at Melody Briggs' research into how children read the Bible. Briggs observed how the children she worked with read the Gospel of Luke with imagination and empathy, encountering it as a story with a clear plot. She concluded that children participate in 'text-reader transactions that produce inside experience of the text'.[18] In the next chapter, we will unpack this further in relation to being present to our congregations. The choice of looking at how children read is deliberate. It is a ringing endorsement of the value of pre-critical readings and reminds people of earlier reading practices that have been squeezed out through training. Once the dolly pegs come out of the bag, most of the students are eager to begin the task. The results are always creative and very often inspiring.

The instructions for each group are straightforward. They are to create, explore and participate in reading a three-dimensional 'living' version of their text, paying attention to what they notice and what they think the text might mean. One of the passages we ask students to explore is Mark 7.1–8.

> Now when the Pharisees and some of the scribes who had come from Jerusalem gathered around him, they noticed that some of his disciples were eating with defiled hands, that is, without washing them. (For the Pharisees, and all the Jews, do not eat unless they thoroughly wash their hands, thus observing the tradition of the elders; and they do not eat anything from the market unless they wash it; and there are also many other traditions that they observe, the washing of cups, pots, and bronze kettles.) So the Pharisees and the

scribes asked him, 'Why do your disciples not live according to the tradition of the elders, but eat with defiled hands?' He said to them, 'Isaiah prophesied rightly about you hypocrites, as it is written,
> "This people honours me with their lips,
> but their hearts are far from me;
> in vain do they worship me,
> teaching human precepts as doctrines."

You abandon the commandment of God and hold to human tradition.'

For this exercise to be of most value, it helps when the ordinands make a note of every choice they make in creating their text. For example, some will begin by reading around this passage and refer back to chapter 6 to work out where it is located so that they can create a backdrop for their characters. Others will make a note of questions they want to take to commentaries and secondary sources about the traditions being described. Others still noted words where they wanted to check the English translation against the Greek. All of these thoughts and interests are worth recording to gain understanding of our instincts and priorities as interpreters. However, the first priority in this exercise is to create the scene itself.

I (Matt) love watching the groups start to create their version of the text. Most of them spend some time near the beginning of the task attempting to identify the characters in the text who might require a dolly peg to represent them. This particular passage presents an interesting case as it contains the editorial notes from the author. A couple of groups in the past have included 'Mark' in the scene. The bit I find most interesting is what people do with the dolly pegs. The positioning of the people in the scene is very telling in terms of how one imagines the event described. Firstly, it is only some of Jesus' disciples who eat with defiled hands yet in every iteration of this exercise the disciples were grouped together, symbolizing solidarity. Quite often, in the three-dimensional representations created by the students, Jesus was placed between the disciples and the Pharisees and scribes to indicate his defence of them. One group took time to draw facial expressions on their dolly pegs, providing a rationale for their decisions, including a frankly cheesed-off Jesus (who, in Mark's Gospel, has just fed the five thousand, walked on water and healed a bunch of people) finding that he is being quizzed about why some of his disciples hadn't washed their hands!

The scenes created often striking visual representations of the creativity and imagination with which we read the text. After each group had presented their take on the passage they had been given they were asked to consider where they were in relation to their scene by exploring these questions:

- Was there a dolly peg with your name on? If so, where were you in the scene?
- Were you seeing the story through the eyes of one of the characters? If so, which one/s?
- Were you sat with an omniscient narrator outside of the scene? If so, why?

Every time I take part in exercises like this, I learn new things about just how I read the biblical text.

Liz has also done this exercise with people training for licensed lay ministry. In her class the group were asked to work with the parable of the Good Samaritan. Neither group included Jesus or his questioner in their scene. At first sight, the illustrations were a bit unimaginative, and simply retold the ubiquitous tale of a kind outsider. One group, though, did include the victim in their scene – a peg lying down and covered in red-ink markings. We reflected on the image for a while and then Liz asked: 'Where is God in this?' A member of the other group, pointed to the injured 'man', and said: 'There.' A hush fell across the room as realization dawned – not only did the exercise work, but it revealed something of God that most of us had not seen before.

Being present to the biblical text in these ways allows us to bring to our reading of scripture who we are in the reality of life. Below is a poetic reflection, written by Tim Watson, a poet, liturgist and priest based in Staffordshire. Tim often finds that being a poet and a preacher overlap. Wrestling with the reality of repeated covid funerals and a sense of the closeness of death in a cold winter season, Tim found himself wondering where Christ is in the midst of the pandemic. He came to re-explore the story of Lazarus in John 11. Being present to the text meant consciously attending to his lived experience and what might have been the lived experience of those in the crowd who watched on. Tim writes:

> The reflection is a cry to an unnamed Jesus. It first acknowledges the common experience of every human facing up to mortality, a truth made to feel ever more real for those witnessing the resuscitation of Lazarus and for us as we live out our lives in the midst of the pandemic. The cry invokes the name of Lazarus and in a movement towards the existential commonality of all people seeks to voice the unspoken angst: 'when you called out his name in grief' and 'were you crying for us all?' is this new life just for Lazarus, or is there hope for the rest of us?

Save us
From the inevitability of death
From the failures we still have left
Save us from ourselves
With each of our remaining breaths
With each second drawing nearer
Each hour passing by
The days that burn with brightness
And months lost in the blinking of all eyes
For the future calls us onward
There's no stopping that direction
No turning back and no reverse
Save us from the notion
Save us from our curse
When you called out the name of Lazarus
And woke him from his death
Aware of the closeness
When the stone was rolled away

The tomb became a font
And called us further forward
For we've all gazed at that void
And faced the ghosts within
We've all held the hand of chaos
Rejected with chagrin
The nights rumble on so lonely
So cold and dark and long
We imagine a silent rhythm
Calling us forward in its song
To dance and step in unison
Perichoresis in action
We've all stared in that direction
And no doubt wondered why
When you called his name in grief
When you called his name in love
When you called his name in loss
When you called his name in tears
Were you crying for us all?
Were you crying for our failings?
Were you crying for our shame?
Were you crying out of pity?
And would we have done the same?
(Tim Watson © 2021)

Getting stuck? Taking a look at examples

So far we have assumed preaching that uses only one passage of Scripture. In churches that follow the Lectionary we might be expected to use more than one Bible reading, finding the links between them. It's a different skill, and we offer two examples below. In the first, the main content was based on the Gospel reading but the sermon as a whole, with its use of an icon of Christ, was written to ensure that the other lections were in the frame. In the second example, I (Liz) brought the congregation into my struggle. They would have made the same assumptions, because the sermon in that church is always based on the

PRESENT TO THE BIBLE

Gospel. I was fairly sure that they would look down on a guilty Herod, and from the vantage point of assumed innocence. I tried to unsettle their comfortable assumptions, and intrigue them a bit, before moving into what is basically a Lenten call to repentance.

Example 1

Joel Love, a priest based in Kent who has a background in linguistics, approached his sermon for midnight communion by creating a sound poem from the words of John 1.1–5. The sound poem was read as below, before the talk progressed with the text that follows. I (Matt) have included all of Joel's talk here with his kind permission. I recommend reading it out loud or asking someone to do that for you. It is written for the ear. It was a stunningly creative way of approaching one of the readings that can feel a bit too familiar for those who regularly attend midnight communion. It also was a way of handling the text through being really present to it.

Sermon for Midnight Mass, 24 December 2020
Preacher: Joel Love
Texts: Isaiah 52.7–10; Hebrews 1.1–4; John 1.1–14

In the Name of the Father and of the Son and of the Holy Spirit. Amen

Icon of Jesus clearly visible

All, all
And, and, and, and, and
Being, being, being
Beginning, beginning
Came, came, come
Darkness, darkness
Did
God, God, God

Has
He
Him, him, him
In, in, in, in
Into, into, into
It
Life, life
Light, light
Not, not
Of
One
Overcome
People
Shines
The, the, the, the, the, the, the, the, the, the
Thing, things
Through
Was, was, was, was, was, was, was
What
With, with
Without,
Word, Word, Word

I (Joel) will now read the sound poem again, and I encourage you to read it too, if possible with an icon of the Lord in front of you.

Repeat sound poem

There are seventy-one words in the opening paragraph of John's Gospel (at least in the NRSV translation). Words that are in danger of becoming so familiar to us that we stop actually hearing them. This is why I have rearranged them alphabetically into a sound poem, which I have been using as a prayer.

Every one of these words speaks to us about Jesus, the very Word of God. In fact, if you do pray them in front of an icon of our Lord, you will notice that every single one of these words can be applied to Jesus directly.

Obviously, he is 'all, all' and 'God, God, God' (three times). Jesus is 'being', 'beginning', 'light' and 'life'. He 'shines' and 'overcomes'. We know all this, but how often do we really think about what it means for us?

The words that are repeated a lot, like 'and' (5x) or 'the' (10x) reiterate through their repetitions that Jesus brings all things together (and, and, and, and, and) while being himself the one and only (the, the, the, the, the, the, the, the, the, the).

When I read the word 'thing', it reminds me of the incarnation (Jesus becomes a thing like us), but also very starkly of the dead body of Christ being laid in the grave. The word 'without' also has echoes of 'My God, my God, why have you forsaken me?' John's gospel opens with intimations of Holy Week.

The reality of suffering is acknowledged in 'darkness, darkness'. The idea that Jesus is 'people' reminds us that whatever we do to one of the least of these who are members of my family we do also to Jesus himself.

On this night, the words that speak most clearly to our present situation are these: 'came, came, come' and 'with, with'. In the incarnation, God does not remain socially distanced from us. Instead, Jesus chooses to 'bubble' with humans. God spends lockdown with us, as one of us. Only in this way can he be the 'life' and 'light' of all people.

Joel's sound poem is an excellent example of how he, as a preacher, sought to be present to the text. He didn't open it up as scene like the exercise described above, or even unfold it. Instead, he unravelled it and laid out the individual threads which made the familiar weft. When I (Matt) first read what he had written I was impressed. When I heard it read out loud, I realized how as a spoken word it was extremely powerful. I encountered it as a personal declaration of faith which intimated the presence of the living Word.

Example 2

In Lent 2019, the readings presented by the Lectionary for my (Liz) sermon were Luke 13.31–35 and Philippians 3.17—4.1. I could not find a way of bringing the congregation into either text, and so I decided to bring them along on the journey of my sermon planning instead. This is what I said:

To be honest, when I first read our readings for this morning, I assumed I would preach on the passage from the Gospel according to Luke. There's so much to go at there. We have Pharisees, local rulers and Jesus lamenting. It's a challenging passage. These Pharisees are not the villains of the piece, as is so often assumed. They come to warn Jesus about Herod, the local politician. Herod wants to kill Jesus. He had already beheaded John the Baptist for criticizing him. Actually, in Herod's terms, because he thought Jesus was John the Baptist come back to life, we might say he wanted to kill Jesus *again*. Herod lived according to his own rules – anyone who got in the way was quickly dispatched. He got rid of his wife so he could marry his sister-in-law, he colluded in the execution of John, and he spent so much time currying favour with Rome that he made enemies of his closest neighbours, the Syrians. No wonder Jesus refers to him as a fox. Foxes in those days were equated not with cunning but with wanton destruction. When these Pharisees warn Jesus about Herod Jesus simply says 'he knows where to find me.' And gets on with what he was already doing.

And Jesus looks over Jerusalem, where prophets have been persecuted and killed, and where he too will die, and he laments that the people would not turn to him. 'I've wanted to gather you to me like a mother hen gathers her chicks under her wings' he says. I'm not entirely sure how comforting it is when threatened by a fox to be offered protection by a chicken, but nevertheless that is what Jesus does.

So there is much to reflect on in our Gospel reading.

But the more this week has gone on, the more I was drawn to the reading from Paul's letter to the Philippians.

Paul too is lamenting, in this part of his letter. 'Some are living as enemies of the cross of Christ', he writes, with tears.

We might think we can identify one or two of those people after the week we have had.

- Knife crime on the rise.
- A massacre in mosques.
- A government apparently in tatters.

It seems fairly easy to point the finger at those who are living as enemies of the cross. It's other people, surely.

But another news item perhaps points the finger in the opposite direction. School children across the world went on strike to draw attention to a climate problem we should have taken seriously long ago. As someone rightly said, for our today they have given their tomorrow. We too fail to follow the way of the cross.

It's right that we dwell on that for a moment, in this season of Lent, the season of repentance.

It's right that we consider repentance. Not simply the repentance that means bemoaning our shortcomings, but the kind of repentance the New Testament writers had in mind when they used the word – turn round, see things differently, adjust your antennae.

That's what I think Paul had in mind when he wrote to the Philippian church:

Our citizenship is in heaven.

Just as it is in Britain at the moment, the issue of citizenship was a live one in Philippi. In 42 BCE, Philippi was the place where Mark Antony and Octavian defeated Brutus and Cassius, the people who assassinated Julius Caesar. It was a pleasant location, and veterans of the victorious army were settled there. Philippi became a luxury resort for former soldiers who had the privilege of Roman citizenship conferred upon them. Citizenship was a big deal. It included some, and excluded others.

So when Paul writes to the church in Philippi 'our citizenship is in heaven', he was, as he often did, also ruling out something else. 'Our citizenship is in heaven. It is *not* in Rome.' Or, as Jesus seems to say in the Gospel reading – his people, and he, is to be found among the poor rather than the powerful.

For the early church, 'heaven' was never an ethereal paradise to be gained by followers of Christ. Heaven meant the reign of God, the place where God's rule can be seen. Not only that, but heaven was everywhere. If you read the four Gospels and notice *nothing* else, you will not be able to miss the fact that Jesus claims the Kingdom of God is near.

Paul doesn't say 'our citizenship *will be* where God reigns' either. He says it *is* where God reigns.

I think it's another call to repentance – to see things differently.

Despite what we see going on around us, and as bad as things appear, our call as citizens of the kingdom of God is to see where God reigns. To adopt a different perspective.

I find it a very easy step from hearing about the tragedies of knife crime to wondering about 'the young people of today'. An easy step, but a wrong one. Most of the young people of today are wonderful, caring, concerned about the world.

It's been pretty easy this week to wonder what on earth our Members of Parliament are up to. Yet the ones I have met have been dedicated, hardworking and trying to do their best for the country.

I don't want to be trite, please don't hear me sweeping difficult topics under some theological carpet where they can be safely ignored. The world is a difficult and painful place. But there is also goodness and beauty and the reign of God in it.

If we do nothing else this Lent, let's try to realize that each day. Having citizenship in heaven might at least mean realizing both the good and the bad.

But repentance isn't just about seeing things differently. It's also about doing them differently. Our citizenship in the Kingdom of God calls us not only to see where God is at work, but also to be part of that activity too. There is a choice to be made – whether to bemoan the state of things, or work for their change.

I've struggled with today's readings. In the end I think they tell us that things are not what they seem. They challenge us to live as citizens under God's reign. Living as citizens of the kingdom of God requires both hope and courage: hope to see what might be and courage to live that way now, hope to hear the music of God's kingdom, and courage to dance to it now.

This sermon works on the principles of the Now Homiletic. I shaped it around the congregation I knew. I spoke personally. Standing in Christ I offered a word for that day.

Preaching too soon

I (Liz) was invited to preach on the Sunday after Ascension Day one year. The readings were Luke 24.44–53 and Acts 16.16–40 – Luke's account of Jesus' ascension and his later account of Paul, Silas and himself in Philippi. You may remember that in Philippi a slave girl possessed by a spirit of divination, a goldmine for her owners, follows the apostle through the city shouting: 'These men are slaves of the Most High God, who proclaim to you a way of salvation.'[19] Luke tells us that Paul was 'very much annoyed'[20] and so healed her. Because her owners had lost their money-spinning opportunity, they have Paul and the others arrested and put in prison. An earthquake shakes the jail open, but the apostles refuse to flee and encourage the other prisoners to stay. Paul insists that the magistrates escort them from the jail because he is a Roman citizen.

Being a woman and a feminist theologian, I read the story from the girl's perspective. She is both owned and possessed, valued only for the income she brings. She is unlikely to be responsible for her position. Yet Paul and his entourage walk on by – apparently on more than one occasion, because Luke tells us that 'while she followed Paul and us she would cry out'. Contrast Jesus' parable of the Good Samaritan, with its implied criticism of those who walk by. Moreover, she tells the truth – the men *are* slaves of the 'Most High God who proclaim to you a way of salvation'. In a classic display of victim-blaming, one commentator suggests that the girl's sin is this – she says the apostles declare *a* way of salvation, rather than *the* way of salvation.

The next problem in writing this sermon was the effect of interpreting the girl and the apostles in this way. To most churchgoers Paul is either a hero or a misogynist with little nuanced characterization. How could I take account of that? In some churches the roles of Jesus and Paul seem to be reversed, Paul's writings are treated with more reverence than Jesus' teachings, and Paul is venerated as the great apostle. Since the other reading was about Jesus' ascension I decided to link the two together by means of a common experience – moving house. I found that it wasn't simply a useful illustration, it helped me to understand something new about Luke's record of the early church. They were getting used to being in a new place! They didn't know how everything worked, any more than we do, but they had moved in and were getting acclimatized. Had I not wrestled with this story to uncover the different perspectives, that of the girl and of the early church learning to inhabit its new home, I might have leaped onto the popular bandwagon, and that would have been preaching too soon.

I have an image of the Bible my mother used to read. It was large, black and very worn with use. It contained more than the words of the Bible, however. On some pages there was more commentary than there was Scripture – this type of Bible seems, sadly, to be enjoying something of a resurgence. My mother's was a Scofield Reference Bible. It encouraged her and her friends to take a perceived shortcut to 'meaning' by reading commentary rather than Scripture. There are other dangerous shortcuts that Now preachers need to avoid, such as section headings, and even chapters and verses. The Bible wasn't 'delivered' in bite-sized chunks with brief guidance notes at the top. Taking too much heed of these can only encourage us to preach too soon, to speak before we understand, and ultimately to treat Scripture as a presenter's material instead of God-breathed, life-saving text.

Better than buying a Bible with someone else's notes already in the margins would be making our own notes to keep a record of the ways God has spoken to us. Bible journaling has become popular recently and wide-margined Bibles are available in many forms. These are helpful when they invite encounter with the text, rather than close it down. None of this is new. The spiritual practice of marginalia has been exercised by many through the centuries in Church history. Recent attention has helped to demonstrate its potential. Broderick Greer, an Episcopal priest from Denver, spoke about marginalia as a guest on the popular podcast 'Harry Potter and the Sacred Text'.[21] He shared how his maternal grandmother, Fairy Turner, wrote in the margins of her green King James Version pocket Bible. Her parents had owned their farm in East Texas, which was highly unusual for black descendants of slaves in their generation. They had raised Fairy and her siblings to value education and be highly literate. Writing in the margins of her Bible was a way of claiming the space to wrestle with the text herself. She had created a record of a conversation between her, the text and preachers of the text.[22] Unlike the notes in the Scofield Bible, the margins did not seek to replace the final word, they kept a record of the latest word to leave you seeking more.

Conclusion

Whatever our pre-commitments are in terms of scriptural authority, exegesis is not being done by machines but by us as preachers and human beings. We are, thankfully, not objective and when we share in our preaching what we have read in the Bible it will be because we think it is important, valuable or meaningful. There is nothing neutral about reading the Bible in faith. This is why it is worth wrestling, and noting what destabilizes or pains us, or makes us change tack. We do this confident in God's ability to speak through the scriptures to us now. Critical study of the scriptures, sound doctrine, and an appreciation of church tradition are all useful. As preachers, we need to ensure that these are not being used to create distance between us and the text. We are interested in knowledge *of* the biblical text, more than knowledge *about* the biblical text.[23]

Growing up, one of my (Matt) prized possessions was the

pool table which I kept in my parents' attic. Over time, the cushions on the table became worn in quite a few places. The badly damaged bits were hidden under the cloth and I was never quite sure where they were. Every so often a ball would hit the cushion and instead of proceeding at the expected trajectory it would shoot off at a different angle, occasionally leaving the table itself. This added an element of unpredictability and even danger to the game! When it comes to reading the Bible with our agendas, preconceptions, prejudices and prior understandings, it might feel like what will come out will be a reflection of what we put in. However, my experience has been that sometimes God speaks in an unexpected way and takes my understanding in a whole new direction. I know that I am kidding myself if I ever think I am in control when it comes to the Word of God. Being present to the scriptures is an exercise in truth-telling – being true to the faith as I have received it, being true to myself and being true to others. Ultimately, this means being open to the Spirit of truth every time I take a shot at interpreting the Bible.

Questions for further reflection

- When was the last time you were surprised by what you read in the Bible? What happened and how did you feel?
- What holds you back from fresh encounters with the text?
- Which ways of preaching from a biblical text might you use that you haven't tried before?
- Thinking of God as the one who is 'ever old and ever new', which of these attributes are you most drawn to in your preaching? How does that have an impact on how you preach?

Notes

1 Barbara Brown Taylor, 2014, *Learning to Walk in the Dark*, Kindle Edition, Norwich: Canterbury Press.
2 John of the Cross, *The Dark Night of the Soul*, trans. Peers, EA, 1959, Image Books (PDF available online at https://holybookslichtenbergpress.netdna-ssl.com/wp-content/uploads/Dark-Night-of-the-Soul-Saint-John.pdf accessed 30.4.21).
3 Sydney Carter, 'One more step along the world I go', lyrics taken from the Church of England's Worship Workshop website for schools, https://www.worshipworkshop.org.uk/songs-and-hymns/hymns/one-more-step-along-the-world-i-go/ accessed 30.4.21.
4 The first church does not follow the Lectionary, the second one does.
5 Matthew 2.1–2.
6 The Character Course can be found here: https://www.thecharactercourse.com/ (accessed 30.4.21; it has been made freely available to use and download).
7 Taken from the script for Session Eight on Curiosity, pp. 1–2. The whole script can be found here: https://drive.google.com/file/d/1SUpD5ogXUwtsjPsF42ySA8LDfthJkeNY/view accessed 30.4.21.
8 Script for Session 8, p. 2.
9 Script for Session 8, p. 2.
10 Script for Session 8, pp. 3–4.
11 I encountered Margaret's work at a preaching symposium in Manchester in 2019. She kindly shared her notes from her presentation. This material is also available at https://preachpreach.com
12 Exodus 2.1–3.
13 Cooling highlights Exodus 1.22 in support of the idea that Pharaoh had enlisted all Egyptians to carry out his policy to kill the Hebrew boys.
14 Bakhtin's position as quoted and characterized in K. Vanhoozer, 1998, *Is there a Meaning in this Text?* Leicester: Apollos, IVP, p. 389.
15 N. T. Wright's article summarizing his main approach to scriptural authority written for BioLogos can be found here: https://biologos.org/articles/n-t-wright-on-scripture-and-the-authority-of-god accessed 30.4.21.
16 N. T. Wright unpacks his fuller argument about how 'God's authority' is exercised through the story of scripture in his 2005, *Scripture and the Authority of God*, London: SPCK, pp. 17–19.
17 For example, William Placher talks about this concept of Paul Ricœur's as being 'on the other side of the hermeneutic of suspicion' where stories can be heard and told once more as stories in 'Teaching Christian Theology', in *Teaching Theology & Religion* 1, no. 1 (1998), 36–47, esp. p. 36.

18 Melody R. Briggs, 2017, *How Children Read Biblical Narrative*, Eugene, OR: Wipf and Stock, pp. 129–130.

19 Acts 16.17.

20 Acts 16.18.

21 The podcast can be found here: https://www.harrypottersacredtext.com (accessed 1.5.21).

22 The transcript of the podcast episode featuring Broderick Greer can be found here: https://static1.squarespace.com/static/571a6e39b6aa608067028725/t/5d82f58884be497be561d0f6/1568863625651/HPST+transcript+4.broderick.pdf (accessed 1.5.21).

23 Knowledge of the text is explored in Dorothy Bass, 2016, 'Imagining: Biblical Imagination as a Dimension of Christian Practical Wisdom', in Dorothy C. Bass et al. (eds), *Christian Practical Wisdom: What it is, Why it Matters*, Grand Rapids: Eerdmans, pp. 232–74, p. 236.

5

Present to Our Congregations

LIZ SHERCLIFF AND MATT ALLEN

Discussions among preachers are generally less than minutes old before the attribute of relevance is mentioned and, usually, extolled. 'The best preaching is relevant', we are told, to the accompaniment of sage nods.

I (Liz) have to admit, at that point, to cringing.

What, after all, do we mean by 'relevance'?

'It's the skill of application,' I'm told.

'And what,' I wonder, 'is that?' We submit applications for jobs or grants. The application of a dressing to a wound helps us to heal. We download apps – applications – to our phones and computers. When supervising children's homework we urge careful application to the task. But which of these is like application in a sermon? Are we asking the congregation for something? Helping their wounds heal? Getting them to work better or differently? Encouraging better work? All may be true, of course, but if that constitutes the whole of preaching, we are constantly 'beating the sheep', blaming them for not improving, as a friend of mine once put it.

The discussion progresses in ways I am sure you are well able to imagine. Preachers want what they say to apply to the lives of their hearers. They want to inspire in them the kind of Christian living some might call 'whole life discipleship'. At the end of it all, debate concludes with general agreement that preachers want what they say to make a difference. A difference in the way people live, a difference to the way they feel about their faith, maybe even a difference to them as representatives of the kingdom of God in the wider world. And sometimes it might.

All too often though, we end up drained and disappointed. What we have said seems to change nothing. And we apply to our wounds the universal salve of blaming the congregation. *We* preached our heart out. *They* didn't change.

We, the preachers, seem to be trapped in a cycle of Bible reading, failed application, and congregation blaming that is edifying neither for us nor for the church. Perhaps there is a different way to preach.

Relevance, it seems to me, begins at the heart of a spider's web type structure from which the preacher extrudes threads toward the imagined lives of hearers. 'What might they be doing tomorrow morning? I need to link this to that.' 'This person works on the shop floor. What does this passage say to them?' 'There are so many young mums in church. I'd better find a link.' Worthy as it sounds, most preachers do not know the drudgery of being a full time carer for a dementia patient, or the emotional drain of managing a workforce where there are impending redundancies, or the stress of balancing a family budget declining in value. Too many threads from the centre of the sermon to its intended target are weak or malformed. The relevance web cannot sustain the weight put upon it.

And even where it can, the extruded threads reach only occasional points around the edge of the sermon, missing out most of the surrounding area entirely.

Too much preaching has been based on an, at root, 'preacher knows best' theology. Whether it is that God tells the preacher what to say, and the congregation had better listen, or that the preacher discerns what the congregation needs to hear and is able to say it, once the pulpit steps have been ascended, the human relationship between preacher and hearers seems to disappear. The preacher in the pulpit becomes the sage on the stage, or screen. Yet faith is not a package of knowledge to be handed on by the knowledgeable to the ignorant. Nor is it a set of propositions that must be properly explained and correctly understood. Faith is nourished by encounter with God and with other believers. The preacher's task is to open up space for such meetings.

If a preacher's lament is that people seem not to learn from what is taught, we should not be surprised. Learning is complex. Firstly, adults do not learn because they are taught. Knowledge does not directly have an impact on behaviour. If it did, nobody would smoke, nobody would overeat, nobody would drive above the speed limit, nobody would fight with their spouse. We know smoking is a cause of lung cancer, yet not all stop smoking. They do, however, worry about persistent coughs. Human beings do not behave rationally, and therefore knowing is not enough. When we know something, we may or may not choose to do it. But if we buy into something, if we own it, then we behave accordingly. Preachers need, therefore, not to hand on knowledge, but to offer something that brings people in and changes their lives. As Leonard Sweet wrote in *Giving Blood: a Fresh Paradigm for Preaching*, 'The core issue of preaching is not "getting something said"; it is not even "getting something heard"; it is getting something experienced that can transform your life for God and the gospel'.[1]

Matt spoke earlier about a schoolteacher he loved. She maintained discipline by getting her pupils to reflect on what they were doing and who they were. She was asking them to put themselves into a story – their story. Stories are powerful. Entering stories can enable us to empathize with other ways of living we might never 'actually' experience; it helps us to see others' perspectives. My favourite teacher also taught English. He could make any text live, and because of him I maintain a love of Shakespeare and Jane Austen. Probably the book that had most direct influence on my life, though, was Qaisra Shahraz' *The Holy Woman*.[2] It's the story of a woman who thought her life was settled, her marriage agreed. But when her older brother died, it was decreed that she should become an imam. Shahraz describes the emotional trauma of giving up one thing in order to follow a calling. I think it might have been the start of my call to ordination.

When I think about being present to the congregation, I find myself asking these questions: How do we avoid seeking either to get something said or have something heard? How does preaching lead people into transformative experiences of God? Matt and I share our different responses these questions below.

We end the chapter by revisiting what it means to preach in in the 'now'.

Liz

In his book *The Splash of Words* Mark Oakley relates poetry to faith. Indeed, he makes the case that poetry is the natural language of faith.

I imagine that some people felt a shudder go down their spine at that sentence. Poetry? The language of faith? Poetry is difficult to understand and even harder to write, some might think. Surely neither I nor Mark Oakley think that preachers should be poets?

Actually, I, at least, do.

I don't expect that everyone can be an Auden, or a Thomas, or an Angelou. But I do think words are important. I think language should be used with solicitude. I think we need to be aware of what we say. A few carefully chosen words allow us to say much more than many careless sentences. Much is available to the careful listener. Much can also, of course, be missed. There is work for listeners to do. This, it seems to me, is the antithesis of the simplistic preaching in which some indulge in the hope that each listener might hear the whole sermon. Rather than reducing the message to a single theme, constantly reiterated, the poem mines its topic for greater depth. Poetry has two houses – the 'high culture' mansion, where rhythm and style are important and comprehension less so; and the 'folk culture' pub snug, where wordsmiths say things more entertainingly than is entirely necessary, but are better understood because of it. Preachers, I think belong in the latter. We construct sentences in memorable ways, that stick to our hearers like 'sticky-grass' in country parks.

One example I worked with is this. I was preaching about Vashti, at a women's event. How could I present her as the shoulders on which Esther stood without being dull or sounding like a campaigner rather than a preacher. This is part of what I did:

How many Vashtis are there?
Queens of the castle,
entertaining friends, with fine food and wine
in the luxury of her chambers
while the king feasts and drinks
and boasts
Just tell them.
They like it.

How many Vashtis are there?
Summoned by a drunken
boaster to entertain his friends.
In the raucous hall,
among the boasting kings
who *just tell them.*
She does not go.

If one refuses,
Others might refuse too.
She has to go.
We must
Just tell them.

How many Vashtis are there?
Summoned women.
Expectant men
Defend their right to
Just tell them.
Do not fear not liking it
They will silence me
I am not afraid.

During lockdown and the days of homeschooling, parents and grandparents expended not a few sentences on social media wondering what 'fronted adverbials' might be and why primary school children of a certain age needed to be familiar with them. The answer, I think, was that they don't, and that they can begin to use them without ever being able to define them, by means of the judicious prompt 'Could you make that sentence more interesting?' Making my sentences more interesting is one reason why I (Liz) often try out sermons aloud before preaching them.

But back to relevance. A sermon designed to be relevant comes to an end as the preacher utters their closing 'Amen'. The relevance web is a complete structure. The package of meaning has been constructed and delivered. It is now for the hearers to take home with them the parcel we have given them, that will often remain unopened.

Resonant sermons, however, work differently. They are not presenting to hearers a well founded, usually incontrovertible argument. Rather, they are delivered whole, as pebbles into still ponds. And once delivered they begin to do their work. Resonant sermons are not about shepherding listeners along linear pathways between points in order that they can see how right we are.

Resonant sermons create still spaces and drop pebbles into them.

Throwing the pebble

Not so long ago, I was invited to speak about preaching at a curates' conference. I will not name the diocese involved, but it was not mine. Some of those present were clearly wedded to relevant preaching, so when the conference leader asked them to go outside for a couple of hours and take some photographs related to resonant preaching, one returned with a beautiful picture of ripples on a pond. I and the conference leader commented that it was a great image of what I meant. 'Ah,' said the curate, 'but I threw a pebble in to make the ripples.' 'That', replied my colleague, 'is the point!' Neither ripples on a pond nor resonant sermons just happen. We have to both select and throw the right pebble. So, I want to return to the question: 'What do we think we are doing?'

Throwing stones into water seems to be almost universally intriguing. How big a splash can we make? How many skips across the surface can we achieve? How far can we throw? They are useful questions for us to bear in mind as we prepare resonant sermons. There are sermons that simply try to throw as far as a possible – for example, those that seem mainly to be aimed at people who are not present that day, bemoaning their absence, rather than celebrating those who are present, for example. There are those that skip along the surface of the text, using the Bible as a launch pad for the preacher's own ideas. But sermons that change things take timely aim at a particular spot and launch with dexterity. Those sermons disturb the whole pond, right to the depths and all the way to the edges.

From past experience, both of pebble throwing and preaching, I know that aiming at the shallows makes very little difference to the whole body of water. Similarly, I know that aiming sermons at those around the edges will leave many hearers untouched. One of my training incumbents told me to preach at those with little experience of faith, because experienced Christians should be able to feed themselves. The difficulty is that when we feed ourselves, unchallenged and undisturbed, we tend to read the same things we've always read and interpret the Bible the same way we've always interpreted it. The more undisturbed a body of water is, the more weeds grow from the bottom, thus protecting it from being unsettled.

Sometimes the people who need to hear a word from God might be in the depths themselves. Not necessarily the depths of faith, but the kind of depths where a lifebuoy is needed, or at least something to hang on to while we take a breath and work out what to do. Not so long ago, during a This Time Tomorrow slot[3] someone who works at a university developing algorithms spoke about their work. Apparently, algorithms are unpredictable, and might facilitate the development of artificial intelligence that supersedes human intelligence. What did the sermon offer them? Or what about the woman pregnant with twins, one of whom was so ill-formed it would be born without a full head? How might a sermon help her decide whether to carry both twins to term? Or how might preaching support the parent whose child has just been expelled from school? These are real issues for people in the congregation. Sermons aimed simply at splashing in the shallows will offer them nothing. Shallow preaching serves only one end – to demonstrate that the Bible has nothing to say to people in the depths.

Our preaching, then needs to go deep, in order to disturb the whole pond.

As a listener I want sermons that dive deep into the whole of the Bible, bringing up pearls of great price, as well as knotty old problems of tradition and theology. I want preachers to display their pearls in the light of our political, economic and social life. I want preachers who, because of their own relational faith, can introduce me to God, not simply give me ideas; preachers who can tell me where and how they encounter God; who can take me by the imagination and say: 'come and see a man …' (John 4.29). I want preachers who tell me the truth, instead of making grandiose claims – there's a huge difference between 'God told me' and 'It seems to me'. And I want preachers who live in the same world I do, who can tell the story of faith in ways that resonate with my experience and give me new ways of living. When I arrive at the church building, or enter the church Zoom room, on a Sunday morning, I hope to hear from a preacher whose hope enables them to hear the music of the future, and whose faith gives them courage to dance to it now.[4]

Matt

Being Dogtanian

I was not playing Dogtanian, I *was* Dogtanian and if you wanted to enter my world you needed to join me in the story of this popular 1980s cartoon adaptation of Dumas' classic *The Three Musketeers*. You could be Juliette, one of the Muskehounds or, if you were suitably sized like one of my patient and long-suffering older cousins, you could be Sandy the horse and carry me around on your back for my latest quest.

Now my children are the same age I was then, I see much of this vividly repeated in them. Whether their heads are buried in books, listening to an audio CD in the car, or watching television at home, they are always identifying with different characters. Often they name this out loud: 'I'm Xuli', 'I'm Kian', 'I'm Skye', 'I'm Chase', 'I'm Kwazi', 'I'm Primrose', 'I'm Peso'. They feel with them, fear with them, laugh with them, and love with them. In other words, they *become* them so that they might experience the world of the story and continue the adventures. They imagine new episodes 'in character' as their fictional heroes and friends. When we are passionate about a story, only full immersion into the experience will do. We enter into stories through empathy.

In the last chapter we briefly encountered Melody Briggs' findings about how children read the Bible. Her research showed how empathizing with biblical characters was vital in making sense of narrative; empathy enables readers of any age to interpret biblical stories experientially.[5] It is a common experience to identify with characters and our choices affect how we understand what is in front of us. By identifying with heroes, we make an idealistic empathy choice. Although part of me still wants to insist that I really am Dogtanian, I have to confess that this falls into that category. By empathizing with other characters who are similar to us or with whom we have things in common, we make realistic empathy choices. There are all kinds of factors which affect identification and sometimes we don't even realize what choices we have made.[6]

Reading the Bible with Tanzanian Christians changed the way Mark Allan Powell understood the parable of the Good Samaritan. Every preacher he had encountered in Western churches had unthinkingly presumed to identify with the person in a position to help. In Tanzania, some empathized with the person who was robbed; they saw the parable as being about being able to receive help from anyone without prejudice.[7] Unless we are aware of the empathy choices being made, we will trip over ourselves and our congregations when we preach.

In the previous chapter we looked at the dolly peg exercise

and I shared some of the insights that came out of making a three-dimensional representation of Mark 7.1–8. We recall that some of Jesus' disciples have eaten with unwashed hands, yet Jesus doesn't condemn them. Instead, he springs to their defence. He rounds on their accusers and highlights the hypocrisy of those religious leaders. Research has indicated that clergy, or others who are theologically trained, are likely to read this text, and others like it, empathizing with Jesus.[8] However, laity tend to empathize with other characters, like the disciples or those considered to be 'in the wrong'. What this means is that when clergy preach on this passage having idealistically empathized with Jesus, they assume that it is about us heroically emulating Jesus's actions in some way. However, if our hearers have realistically identified with other characters, they are not going to be immediately tuned in for the talk which is exploring 'how to be more like Jesus'. They are more likely to be asking what this story reveals about what Jesus might be saying to them in their defence, for their protection, or as a rebuke.[9]

Having marked, assessed and offered feedback on hundreds of other people's sermons, I have seen how underestimating the importance of the empathy choices people are making can lead to missed opportunities in preaching. One former student, Steve Murphy, who is a parish priest in the north-west of England, has kindly given me permission to share an example of this in a talk he sent to me for some feedback in the past. The passages were Luke 15.1–10 (The Lost Sheep and the Lost Coin) and 1 Timothy 1.12–17.

The sermon started with a bang as Steve told a gripping story about how he lost the FA Cup. That is, he mislaid the trophy having been put in charge of bringing it to the open top bus being used by Manchester United to parade their success in 1983. In those days long before mobile phones, Steve described how he felt in the two hours when the trophy was missing:

> I was frantic – and what was worse I felt that I couldn't tell anybody about it.
>
> I was a young man just starting out on a career and I didn't

PRESENT TO OUR CONGREGATIONS

want to be defined for the rest of that career as the numpty who'd literally lost the FA Cup. I'd never live that down.

The FA Cup had been in a plain wooden box. A colleague had taken it by mistake and had been driving around with it in their van. Steve described to his hearers the relief he felt at the moment the trophy was discovered.

At this point in the sermon, hearers are empathizing with Steve – the preacher. They are likely recalling that same feeling of losing something precious and perhaps also the experience of when it was found. The preacher has steered the hearers' empathy choices. They have been given a way to identify with him through his personal story and they will follow his lead in making a shift to feel with another who has lost or found something. Everything was set up for hearers to experience Jesus' story through the eyes of the shepherd and the woman of Luke 15. The preacher had prepared a way for them to immerse themselves into the text and ultimately identify with how God might feel in losing and finding. This was a decisive moment in the sermon, so what did Steve do?

Steve began to make links between his story and the Gospel passage: both were powerful stories about losing and finding something. He acknowledged that we lose things which are precious. However, he then moved on quickly to make the general point that stories can be powerful and used that to make links with the second reading. The message of the sermon became that we ought to use our stories to point others to God. Towards the end of the sermon Steve briefly returned to the idea of being lost to encourage us to pray for opportunities to share with others our stories of being found by God. I don't wish to be overly critical. There was a clear logic to the sermon. It was obvious that Steve had thought about how to draw out the points he wanted to make and explain their relevance. However, it didn't connect with all the emotions stirred by his story.

This sermon illustrates how important it is to consider what hearers experience as well as what they hear. It missed the opportunity to work fully with the empathy created at the start of the sermon for those who lose something precious and then find it. As a hearer, I was ready to see myself as the shepherd and the woman of the Bible reading. I felt cued in to reflect on God's heart towards us expressed in the story – frantically searching until the joyful relief of a successful hunt. This would have been a sermon shaped by resonance. The talk was good, but it could have been made better simply by tuning in to the empathy choices of the hearers. Steve's opening story was excellently chosen. It was attention-grabbing and engrossing and brought more to the talk than he first realized. Instead of just telling us to use our stories to point to God, this sermon could be rewritten to show us a powerful example.

Below, I have included a sermon based on John 11 and the raising of Lazarus. In that talk, you can see how I attempted to create space for multiple empathy choices but also steered my hearers' identification to enhance and give shape to their encounter with the biblical text in a way which mirrored my own. My belief is that if we want our preaching to lead people into transformative experiences of God, we need to actually lead the way. That means we need to have gone before and be willing to go again. We have opened the scriptures, thrown ourselves into the story, and have prepared for a return trip where we will be a personal guide and companion to others. We need to be alert to, and make space for, the empathy choices that can be made when we engage with the Bible. We need to be aware of the choices that hearers make while we are preaching. Present preachers know that they are co-readers of the text. Our task is about more than application and relevance. We invite hearers to feel with us as we seek to feel with them at every stage of preaching. We need to show that we can be Dogtanian, Juliette, the Muskehounds and Sandy, too.

A Service of Induction for New Ordinands and Trainee Readers

The Eucharist of All Saints
Preacher: Matt Allen
Texts: Isaiah 25.6-9; John 11.20-44

This summer I heard a story that sounded familiar.
It was the story of a man of legendary status.
His name is well-known.
He is faced with a fatal affliction.
As he passes away the women by his side lay him to rest.
It seemed to all the world that he had died but they dared to hope that this was not the end ...

On holiday several weeks ago, my family and I were staying near Glastonbury where I came across this legend about a great battle of King Arthur.

Arthur had been double-crossed and there was only one solution: to battle against his own son, Mordred. The fighting was fierce and the troop laboured, but eventually Arthur's army were victorious. Yet, somehow in the melee, Arthur becomes separated from his trusted sword, Excalibur. Unarmed, Arthur is attacked and mortally wounded. His life is near its end. As the breath is slowly leaving his body, nine Celtic goddesses come to take him away to the island paradise of Avalon. There they laid him on a golden bed and took up watch over him.

But this is not the end of the story – there is more to come ...

Their watch continues still, for they say King Arthur did not really die – he sleeps! He will stir and return to defend Britain, when Britain has need of him.[10]

Today's Bible readings for this induction service, are those used to celebrate All Saints Day at the start of November. All Saints is a period of time in the Church's calendar when those who have died are remembered and we are reminded that there is one Church across time and space.

We don't pretend that those who have gone before didn't die, like in the legend of King Arthur. Instead, we hold on to the hope that there is more to come.

We try to picture the whole, the total, the *all* and look to a future beyond death and beyond limits.

The familiar Gospel reading picks up this theme. In John 11 we see how Jesus is slow to respond to the news of his friend Lazarus's illness. He goes to the home of Martha, Mary and their brother when it all seems too late.

But there is more to come.

Martha

Martha strides towards Jesus while he is still on his way. Martha is direct and determined. With the fire of faith in her eyes, as they meet, she says: 'Lord, if you had been here, my brother would not have died. But even now I know that God will give you whatever you ask of him.'

With those eyes, Martha sees Jesus as someone with extraordinary access to God. 'God is with you,' said Nicodemus in chapter 3. 'God will give you whatever you ask,' says Martha here. She looks up to him. She looks *to* him.

Sometimes I feel like Martha when I think of those who have led and taught me in the faith, I have at times assumed that they had somehow had extra spiritual authority, that their prayers were worth more. As those training for ministry, I wonder how we might respond when others seem to hold that impression of us?

Here, Martha is the one who expected Jesus to do something; she still expects that Jesus will do something, that there is more to come.

Jesus confirms this, saying to her: 'Your brother will rise again.' Martha agrees, like others in the Jewish religious culture of the time, she believes in a final resurrection on the last day. This is an informed answer. Martha has read Daniel 12. She has read Tom Wright (perhaps not!).

But there is more to come.

Indeed, far more than she has bargained for is standing right in front of her.

She says: 'I believe in the resurrection.'

Jesus says: 'I *am* the Resurrection ... and the Life. Those who believe in me, even though they die, will live, and everyone who lives and believes in me will never die. Do you believe this?'

She says to him, 'Yes, Lord, I believe that you are the Messiah, the Son of God, the one coming into the world.'[11]

I love Martha here!

She expresses bold faith.

She thinks big thoughts.

She knows her own mind.

But then she gets immediately distracted and goes off to call her sister. She doesn't stop long enough to attend to the person in front of her, to listen carefully to Jesus or even reflect on the weight of her own words.

She says such amazing things of Jesus.

She knows such amazing things of Jesus.

Somehow though the things of Jesus seem to get stuck in her mind.

But there is more to come.

Mary

Next, Mary goes to see Jesus, she is the one called by him but a crowd have followed her.

When she sees Jesus, Mary does something different to Martha: she kneels at his feet. Literally, falls at his feet. From that position she says the same words as Martha: 'Lord, if you had been here, my brother would not have died.'[12]

And that's all they say to each other

And she weeps.

And others weep.

And Jesus is greatly disturbed in spirit and deeply moved

And Jesus weeps.

For all the mentions of death today, we have not spoken of the reality of personal loss, grief, bereavement. The things we see when we really attend to each other and enter into the pain felt among human communities. Nothing in this story minimizes what is commonly and keenly felt when our loved ones die.

As I see Mary weeping, each sob seems to express a deep knowing. Wordless utterances of wisdom from a spirit infused with faith.

I wonder if she weeps only for her own loss or does she also have an eye on the crowd. Does she sense how things might turn against Jesus? At the start of chapter 12, it is this Mary who will anoint Jesus' feet.

Sometimes, I feel like Mary, when I am not ready to put what I know into words or explain it to others and try to express it through action.

The things of Jesus are hidden in her heart.

But there is more to come.

Lazarus

Our final scene happens at the place where Lazarus is confined.

Upon arrival, Jesus asks for the stone to be moved with a promise of seeing the glory of God, if you believe.

As the light floods into the tomb, Jesus prays out loud to God his Father.

His prayer shows to the crowd that it is more important who he is, not what he does. This is a prayer of thanks, for God has already heard him. Even as Jesus speaks, Lazarus is stirring, but it remains to be seen.

And it needs to be seen because this is more than a legend, more than a miracle, this is a sign.

A sign of the more that is to come in the story of Jesus.

A sign of what it will mean.

A sign that the Resurrection and the Life will, in the words of Isaiah, destroy the shroud and swallow up death for ever.

Here today as 'All Saints', we are part of that bigger story. We do not think that we have the whole picture, but we are going to share what we have and what we bring while we look for what lies beyond us.

Today is not the end, but a new beginning.

Today, we hold on to the hope that there is more to come, and

Today, we are being stirred by Jesus.

Maybe, like Martha, the things of Jesus get stuck 'up here' (*pointing to the head*).

Maybe, like Mary, the things of Jesus become hidden 'in here' (*hand on heart*).

Maybe faith has felt stone cold dead (*arms tightly folded*).

Jesus calls to all of us like he did to Lazarus. His voice bounces back from the tomb.

And Jesus says: Come Out! (*hand gesture beckoning them to come*)

Now, Fleabag

Back in Chapter 1 we saw the huge contribution of the New Homiletic in asserting the sermon as an event. It encouraged the kind of preaching that would have bags of potential to be resonant rather than relevant. It invited attention to language, form and aesthetics. It traded in metaphor, imagination and story. Active participation was in its DNA. Its aim was to fuse the horizons between the congregation and the biblical text: preachers would serve up a narrative banquet, a feast for the senses, in which hearers would encounter God. It sounds like a dream, but, as we saw, this kind of preaching can turn into a nightmare. When preachers become imaginers for hire, preaching resonant sermons, we might stop being present to our congregations.

In recent years, on more than one occasion, people have described some of my better preaching as 'spellbinding' and 'beguiling' when thanking me for a sermon. I (Matt) admit to being pleased with that response. Like most preachers, I enjoy writing talks that move others. It is nice to hear feedback which is intended to be encouraging. However, these words indicate something which should give me cause for concern. There is a real risk that I might slip into patterns of preaching packed with imagination and inspiration, but where the real 'me' takes hold of a mask and hides. Far too often in my preaching I avoid doing the one thing I know is most important – to speak personally as someone 'in Christ'. It is far easier to focus on spinning a web or weaving a yarn for others, even when beginning with the best of intentions. For resonant preaching to have integrity it must contain personal speech and for personal speech to remain resonant we must have integrity. If trying to preach without authority was the problem of the New Homiletic, striving to preach with integrity is the challenge of the Now Homiletic.

If we want to speak with authority, we need to be present and real.[13] As we saw in Chapter 1, Paul's Second Letter to the Corinthians helps us to get to grips with what this looks like. In 2 Corinthians 4.2 we read the following:

> We have renounced the shameful things that one hides; we refuse to practise cunning or to falsify God's word; but by the open statement of the truth we commend ourselves to the conscience of everyone in the sight of God.

Paul is building towards his image of the clay jars where those who are 'in Christ' are described as ordinary pieces of earthenware who contain God's treasure. Here, Paul talks about the open statement of the truth. The Greek word translated as 'open statement' literally means 'manifestation' and can mean embodying or making visible. This is contrasted with cunning or craftiness where motives are being concealed.[14] This is about more than the content of what is being said. Preaching with integrity is like the hokey-cokey – you put your whole self in. This is a challenge I want to take seriously but I don't want to give up on preaching sermons shaped by the New Homiletic – sermons that use narrative and create storied worlds for my hearers to experience. I think we can do both and I found inspiration in an unlikely place: *Fleabag*.

I am an avid viewer of television box sets and have often wondered about the many ways in which this hobby informs and shapes my instincts as a preacher. In 2016, while eagerly anticipating the start of a new season of the US version of television show *House of Cards*, I encountered an article titled '15 TV Shows that Broke the Fourth Wall'.[15] It listed some of the television shows since the 1990s to feature actors who break the 'golden rule' by looking at the camera. In other words, they addressed or acknowledged the existence of the audience.[16] These characters play a role in the unfolding narrative and they step outside the timeline of that narrative, perhaps just momentarily, to offer comments from their perspective 'directly' to the viewer. More recently, BBC comedy *Fleabag* has employed the same technique, which I will refer to as 'direct address'.[17] *Fleabag* is not everyone's cup of tea and Fleabag herself (the titular character) is no role model. However, there is something about the use of direct address in *Fleabag* which I think is useful to preachers.

Before exploring *Fleabag*, it is worth taking a look at direct address – a powerful tool that bucks the trend of most of the things we watch on screen. Usually, we are taken into a world created by the story being told. This world is known as its *diegesis*.[18] The convention that emerged in film in the twentieth century was that viewers would watch the story unfold entirely within the diegetic world in which the camera seems not to exist.[19] Actors were not to directly address the audience as it would destroy the 'hypnotic illusion'.[20] Viewers become voyeurs who are hidden away, benefitting from the access and power of the camera.[21] At the same time as the New Homiletic in preaching, a movement known as 1970s Screen Theory set its sights on challenging voyeuristic cinema and its hypnotic illusion.[22] Inspiration for this came from the theatre. Bertolt Brecht is a key voice who sought to bring together the story and the audience. Brecht was committed to anti-illusionism which is about breaking the seal of the story world to expose the forces at work behind the scenes.[23] Direct address does this.

It invites a different kind of relationship with an audience. It implies a desire to be present and to be real about the story being told.[24]

Fleabag is a situation comedy about the life, loves and losses of the main character – 'Fleabag'. Fleabag is a white Londoner in her late twenties. Right from the beginning of the first episode, a personal relationship is established between this character and the audience because she breaks the fourth wall to directly address us, the viewers.[25] Fleabag draws us in by offering us extra information as an aside, sharing inappropriate levels of detail about her relationships, and by keeping in touch with us through eye-contact.[26] Fleabag knows the viewer is watching her and seems to enjoy the attention of the camera. She shows she is in charge of events by predicting the actions of others and sharing inside jokes with the viewer.[27] Fleabag looks like she is being open and honest with us, until we discover her betrayal of a friend and realize that she has only shown us a limited version of the truth.[28] From then on, in that episode, she avoids the camera and no longer seeks to address us.[29] *Fleabag* reminds us that direct address is risky. It does not confer power and control: it invites scrutiny and it exposes inauthenticity. Fleabag broke the fourth wall to be present, but we discovered that she was not being real.

Fleabag is a model for preaching and warning for preachers. Preaching now includes far more speaking through screens than it used to. When our hearers are not gathered within the same space for a shared act of worship, we need to break the fourth wall to be present to them. Shows which use direct address like *Fleabag* illustrate how to do this. We can tell a story *and* make room for honest commentary where we speak personally. This however comes with a warning. Speaking personally is not about filling sermons with the poorly judged or distracting personal stories preachers sometimes tell. Speaking personally is about taking opportunities to be present, to be real. In other words, we drop all the masks and show that we are interested in or even irritated by what we are sharing.

The world of the text is neither hermetically sealed nor tame. Our hearers are not voyeurs but conscious observers and co-sojourners in that unfamiliar world. They look to the preacher for guidance, but also encounter revelation themselves. When we pause the story and give a glimpse behind the scenes, preachers can grab their hearers' attention and heighten their observation. The preacher's self-disclosure is not an end itself, but only a means for speaking honestly about their encounter with God through the text and the larger biblical story. In other words, instead of telling others how what we are saying might be relevant to them, we are showing what has already resonated with us and throwing it open to them. To do this honestly means accepting that our knowledge is always partial. What I notice and experience in the world of the biblical text is shaped by who I am and what I believe I will find there. I am not objective about what I preach and what I bear witness to is always larger than my experience of it. Fleabag's story reminds us that God's story is bigger than any preacher's; if we gloss over the challenges of faith or act like we have it all under control then we will fail to be real.

The New Homiletic highlighted the limitations of speaking 'in role'. The Now Homiletic highlights the possibilities of speaking 'in person' and not hiding behind the stories we tell. The use of direct address in *Fleabag* illustrates how preachers can be inspired to reclaim their authority to preach, but only confident of our right to do so if we are going to speak personally, telling the truth. Before I get accused of 'Preaching the Gospel according to Fleabag' I want to highlight how the same approach can be found in the scriptures. The Gospel writers make use of the perspective of a narrator. John regularly brings in and silences the voice of the narrator as characters converse and interact.[30] John's Gospel was probably written to be read aloud in liturgical settings.[31] With his comments, asides and occasional direct address (e.g. John 20.31), John and *Fleabag* have more in common than we might think!

Now, not then

If the New Homiletic was concerned with fusing the horizons of text and congregation, the Now Homiletic is aimed at bringing the congregation into a story that is already theirs. I (Liz) mentioned holistic time in Chapter 2, with the reminder that when we worship God we join a stream of worship that has been taking place for millennia. We are not taking a story from the Bible and joining it, or applying it to our story. The Bible's story is ours. One of the best symbols of Christian hospitality is the table, so let's begin there. When we gather to share in Communion, bread and wine are shared. It is intended to be a visceral experience. In *take this bread*, Sarah Miles writes:

> One early, cloudy morning when I was forty-six, I walked into a church, ate a piece of bread, took a sip of wine. A routine Sunday activity for tens of millions of Americans – except that up until that morning I'd led a thoroughly secular life, at best indifferent to religion, more often appalled by its fundamentalist crusades. This was my first communion. It changed everything.[32]

No theological explanation, no clear expression of faith, joining the story of faith by joining its telling changed Sarah's life. Similarly, on the night before he died, Jesus did not give his disciples a three-point, alliterated sermon on what the meal or his coming death meant. He shared food with them. It was a Passover meal; they were engaging in collective remembrance. Sarah's communion wasn't about something that had happened; Jesus' celebration of Passover wasn't about something that would happen. Each event also happened 'now'.

A short passage from Deuteronomy will help explain the point:

> A wandering Aramean was my ancestor; he went down into Egypt and lived there as an alien, few in number, and there he became a great nation, mighty and populous. When the Egyptians treated us harshly and afflicted us, by imposing

hard labour on us, we cried to the LORD, the God of our ancestors; the LORD heard our voice and saw our affliction, our toil, and our oppression. (Deuteronomy 26.5–7)

The speaker begins by looking back to the times of their father, the wandering Aramean. But in verse 6 the story becomes his also 'the Egyptians treated *us* harshly'; '*we* cried to the Lord'. The narrator enters into collective remembrance, just as we do at the Communion table, and just as we do in Now Preaching.

Now Preaching is a great balancer in how we speak to our congregations. By entering into a shared narrative we avoid the easy (and false) distinction between Old Testament Law and New Testament Grace, because it's all the same story – ours, now. Our shared narrative binds us to those who have gone ahead of us, not just within the Christian tradition but throughout the history of God's outreaching to humanity. A wandering Aramean was our father, and we too cried out to God when the Egyptians – and the slave-traders, and the racists, and every other oppressor through the ages – afflicted us.

Secondly, the Law is living and responsive. It has never offered an off-the-peg solution to life's problems, be they personal, communal, national or global. It is for us to interpret and explore in light of the present. As preachers it is never open for us to pronounce in authoritarian tones what the Law back then said – it speaks now.

The Now Homiletic liberates and enlivens both Law and Grace, both Testaments, our shared narrative. Just as Ruth says to Naomi 'Your people shall be my people, and your God my God' (Ruth 1.16), so the Now Preacher invites hearers into a joint heritage that reaches both back and forward in time, but coalesces now.

Holding back the 'we'

Throughout this book Liz and I (Matt) have been careful to own our own voices. This has been deliberate so that we could address you, the reader, as ourselves and be clear about who was saying what. We have had to think about when to use the word 'we' and it helped us to realize how important it is to also do this when preaching. Holding back the 'we' is important when a relationship is being established between the speaker and the hearer. Often the advice to those sharing a thought for the day on the radio is to use 'you' and 'I' rather than 'we'. 'We' can stop us being present when it means failing to own our own thinking or generalizing the experience of others.[33] I think it is okay to use 'we' when it expresses our solidarity and togetherness, indicates that the gospel addresses more than what is personal (for example, social justice),[34] or refers to something which has definitely been a shared experience (like the Bible reading that 'we' heard just before the talk). There is a place for 'we' to express unity. However, at other times, deliberately using 'you' and 'I' might be more effective in helping us to identify with others and enable the 'we' to stand out more effectively. During lockdown, pre-recording sermons, I have been thinking about how I make choices in this area. In the example below, despite recording the talk four days before the service was streamed, I sought to be present to the congregation by holding back the 'we'.

Talk for Sunday 10 January 2021, a few days after the third national lockdown was announced in the United Kingdom

Reading: Matthew 4.1–11
Preacher: Matt Allen

I don't think that you need me to tell you the significance of this past week. For some, this is a time of suffering. For others, it may feel like a time of testing.

Today, in our reading, we see Jesus being tested. You probably know the story, but if you're anything like me right now the last thing you need to get from this a tonne more information or advice to follow. I want to go deeper and get to the heart of what is going on.

Matthew's Gospel tells us right at the start what it is about. It begins in Matthew 1.1 where it describes itself as 'an account of the genealogy of Jesus the Messiah'. In Greek, it is *Biblos geneseōs Iēsou Christou* – the book of the origin of Jesus Christ.[35]

Biblos geneseōs might sound a bit familiar. It is the Greek name for the book of Genesis.

Matthew is telling us about a new genesis, a new world, a new creation all focussed on Jesus. It is as though, throughout his book, Matthew is asking us one question.

A question that comes into sharp focus in our reading today.

A question that speaks to our lives right now:

'Do you see where Jesus is coming from?'

'Do you see where Jesus is coming from?'

I love Matthew's Gospel. It is systematic and consistent. There are five blocks of teachings. They match the first five books of the Old Testament, known as the Pentateuch.

At the very start of the Gospel, Matthew is bringing out all of the classics: Jesus is an unexpected child of Abraham; as a baby, like Moses, Jesus escapes the clutches of a tyrant ruler; like Israel, Jesus is the beloved Son of God brought out of Egypt; Jesus passes through the waters of baptism; and Jesus is led by the Spirit or presence of God into the wilderness to be tested.

In Jesus, something old is being awoken; something new has begun.

Three whole chapters have gone by before today's reading, but the adult Jesus hasn't really done much. There has only been one scene of any note. Jesus has said one thing. It was in last week's reading. When John the Baptist tried to protest against baptizing Jesus in chapter 3, Jesus answered: 'Let it be so now; for it is proper for us in this way to fulfil all righteousness.'[36]

Jesus has made clear the importance of fulfilling all righteousness: doing what is right ourselves; making possible what is right for everyone.

And he's right – when Jesus came up from the water, a voice from heaven said, 'This is my Son, the Beloved, with whom I am well pleased.'[37]

Do you see where Jesus is coming from?

With the voice still ringing in his ears, Jesus is led by the Spirit into the wilderness.

Then the days start to pass and perhaps that voice starts to fade

1 day

2 days

10 days

20 days

40 days with no food. He is hungry and weary. Weak, gaunt and skeletal, his eyes that once seemed to sparkle have dulled. The reserves are gone.

Jesus is going through the experience of the Israelites In Deuteronomy 6—8 (read these scriptures together if you want to dig deeper). After knowing God's saving action, they were led there 'on a high'. They were meant to be there to be tested and formed as God's people. But Israel stepped out into the wilderness and forgot who they were. Healthy doubts and openness of spirit became dullness of heart in the heat of the desert.

How will Jesus fare in the face of the same temptation?

Back in the story, it begins with a new voice – a voice that is not from heaven. Everything that the voice told Jesus to do would make Jesus focus on his needs, his wants, his reputation.

In the first temptation – turn these stones into bread – the voice says: 'Serve yourself!'

In the second temptation – making a scene to show off – the voice says: 'Prove yourself!'

The third temptation – claim power and prestige – the voice says: 'Honour yourself!'

I know I hear the same kind of message:

'Assert yourself.'

'Treat yourself.'

'Enjoy yourself.'

'Please yourself.'

'Express yourself.'

'Suit yourself.'

It's not that these things are always wrong on their own, but Jesus is not going to let history repeat itself.

He will show what it looks like to keep trusting in God for our needs so that we can meet each other's needs.

Do you see where Jesus is coming from?

As Jesus resists temptation, what stands out to me most is that I am not like Jesus. It is my story, it is our story, that we do not always resist temptation. We have our prices, our vices, and a tipping point.

Once the right offer is on the table it will trigger a desire to have and hold.

I wonder how much energy I have spent on trying to find and maintain my own comfort, to avoid pain, to avoid suffering.

The tempter is pretty reasonable at first, pretty convincing. Conventional wisdom would even seem to be on his side. 'Look after number one first,' he says. But Jesus doesn't just reject the offers put in front of him. Jesus rejects conventional wisdom.

All that Jesus will be about will be about more than life as we know it. Jesus has a deeper sense of what is real. Jesus knows that what God has for humanity is more than human beings want from God – not domination of the kingdoms of the world, but dominion over all creation as part of a relationship of trust in the rule and reign of God.

Do you see where Jesus is coming from?

In this story there is a clash of values and the clash of kingdoms that will play out across the whole Gospel.

Did you notice how the testing literally escalates? It keeps going up.

It starts in the wilderness. The tempter invites him to focus on what will keep him alive, but Jesus would rather speak of the one who brings us to life.

It moves up. The tempter takes him to the top of the temple. But Jesus is more about going to the houses and streets.

Then they go further up to a high mountain. The tempter promises all the kingdoms of the world. But you ain't gonna get anywhere with Jesus no matter how high you raise the stakes!

Because everything that Jesus is about in Matthew's Gospel is the Kingdom of heaven that comes down. It comes down. It is down, now.

Even when we can't see it, it is working from below and transforming from within.

'The kingdom of heaven is like yeast.'

'The kingdom of heaven is like a mustard seed.'

'The kingdom of heaven is like treasure hidden in a field.'[38]

Do you see where Jesus is coming from?

'The Kingdom of heaven has suffered violence, and the violent take it by force.'[39] Yet it is at hand. It belongs to the poor in spirit, to the children, to 'those who are persecuted for the sake of righteousness'.[40]

Do you see where Jesus is coming from?

He is the one fulfilling all righteousness.

And that is:

Not about getting ahead of yourself, but about getting behind others.

Not about climbing up, but about reaching down.

Not about holding on, but about letting go.

To do what is right ourselves. To make possible what is right for everyone.

Jesus' experience in the wilderness gives him every right to preach the sermon he is about to give on the mountain.

'Blessed are those who hunger and thirst for righteousness.'

'Blessed are those who are persecuted for righteousness' sake.'

'Seek first the kingdom of God and his righteousness, and all these things will be given to you as well.'[41]

After Jesus dismisses the accuser, all that he had turned down is given to him: food, the help of angels, and in time rule and authority of earth and heaven. There is surely hope to come.

Pause

But before that, there is a journey ahead. The voice that here says: 'serve yourself', 'prove yourself', 'honour yourself', will later turn into the taunts at the cross: 'Save yourself.' 'Save yourself.'

The one lifted up to see the kingdoms of the world will be lifted up to expose the futility of the world, its vanity and emptiness, its fragility, its 'self'.

At the start of this new year, this new lockdown, as this hits home I ask:
'Where am I coming from?'
'Where are you coming from?'
Do we see where Jesus is coming from?

Questions for further reflection

- Can you think of a time you preached a sermon which resonated with people in different ways? What do you think particularly helped it to speak to others?
- As you prepare a sermon, how might you consider the empathy choices of your hearers?
- What reasons might a preacher have for 'breaking the fourth wall'?
- What do you think about the use of 'we' in the example sermon? What might you do differently in your preaching as a result of exploring this idea?
- How could you make your sermons more poetic? Take the last one you preached and rewrite some of it so that it is more poetic, revealing more of how you feel and engaging with hearers now.

Notes

1 L. Sweet, 2014, *Giving Blood: A Fresh Paradigm for Preaching*, Grand Rapids: Zondervan, p. 49.

2 Q. Shahraz, 2001, *The Holy Woman*, Arcadia Books.

3 This is a slot during service when a member of the congregation talks about what they will be doing 'this time tomorrow'.

4 'Hope is the ability to hear the music of the future. Faith is the courage to dance to it in the present.' (Attributed to Peter Kuzmic, a Croatian theologian and evangelist who teaches at Gordon-Conwell Theological Seminary.)

5 Melody R. Briggs, 2017, *How Children Read Biblical Narrative*, Eugene, OR: Wipf and Stock, p. 186.

6 Mark A. Powell, 2001, *Chasing the Eastern Star: Adventures in Biblical Reader-Response Criticism*, Louisville, KY: Westminster John Knox Press, pp. 20–21.

7 For more on this example see Powell, *Chasing the Eastern Star*, pp. 20–21.

8 For a detailed exploration of Allan Powell's research see Mark A. Powell, 2007, *What Do They Hear? Bridging the Gap between Pulpit and Pew*, Nashville, TN: Abingdon Press.

9 Powell, *What Do They Hear?*, pp. 55–60.

10 I also read a version of the story from this internet resource: https://www.timelessmyths.com/arthurian/mortartu.html (accessed 3.5.21).

11 Martha and Jesus' exchange is from John 11.21–27.

12 John 11.32.

13 Kate Bruce suggests that the preacher's integrity offers a basis for their authority and writes that 'there is no place for authoritarian hectoring that seeks to enforce conformity and crush dissent', but there is 'a place for authoritative monologue' which 'authentic, open and honest', in Kate Bruce and Jamie Harrison (eds), 2017, *Wrestling with the Word: Preaching Tricky Texts*, London: SPCK, Location 308.

14 The Greek word *panourgia* indicates something inherently negative and dishonest in the New Testament. Cf. 2 Corinthians 11.3 where it is linked with the serpent in the Genesis narrative and Ephesians 4.14 where it supports the notion of deceitfulness. In Luke 20.23, it is used in the coin incident with the Herodians and Pharisees.

15 Kat Sommers, 2016, '15 TV Shows that Broke the Fourth Wall', Anglophenia, BBC America. https://www.bbcamerica.com/anglophenia/2016/03/15-tv-shows-that-broke-the-fourth-wall accessed 3.5.21.

16 Sommers, '15'.

17 This choice follows Tom Brown whose rationale for using the term is partly pragmatic. Brown takes a detailed look at the use of direct address in cinema, noting that it is distinctive from both television and theatre. However, I contend that some of the principles behind its use in cinema are evident in *Fleabag* and can safely be assumed to share some commonality across media in their handling of narrative. To explore this further, see T. Brown, 2012, *Breaking the Fourth Wall: Direct Address in the Cinema*, Edinburgh: Edinburgh University Press, p. x.

18 Emphasis mine. Claudia Rapp has explored this same term in the Bible, for example in the opening sentences to Luke's Gospel, 'Storytelling as Spiritual Communication in Early Greek Hagiography: The Use of Diegesis', *Journal of Early Christian Studies* 6, 3 (1998), pp. 431–48, pp. 444–45.

19 Brown recognizes that this is all very slippery ground in terms of what is really 'real', in Brown, *Breaking*, pp. xi–xii.

20 Frank Woods as cited in Brown, *Breaking*, p. 4.

21 Tom Gunning, 1994, *D. W. Griffith and the Origins of American Narrative Film: The Early Years at Biograph*, Urbana, IL: University of Illinois Press, p. 262.

22 Brown, *Breaking*, 6.

23 Brown, *Breaking*, 10.

24 Brown cautions against over-simplifying or caricaturing 1970s Screen Theory. He describes the adoption of direct address by some who sought to reveal and resist the structures of representation in cinema: Brown, *Breaking*, p. 7.

25 Faye Woods, 'Too Close for Comfort: Direct Address and the Affective Pull of the Confessional Comic Woman in *Chewing Gum* and *Fleabag*', *Communication, Culture & Critique* 12 (2019), pp. 194–212, esp. p. 195.

26 Woods, 'Too Close', p. 204.

27 Woods, 'Too Close', p. 207.

28 Woods, 'Too Close', p. 210.

29 Woods, 'Too Close', p. 210.

30 George Parsenios identifies two commonly cited examples of this in John 3 (Parsenios, 'Anamnesis and the Silent Narrator in Plato and John', *Religions* 8 (2017), pp. 1–11, especially pp. 1–2).

31 Aileen Guilding suggests that John may have been writing to preserve the style of 'synagogue sermons': Guilding, 1960, *The Fourth Gospel and Jewish Worship*, Oxford: Clarendon, p. 57.

32 S. Miles, 2012, *Take this Bread: A Radical Conversion*, Norwich: Canterbury Press, p. xi.

33 Jennifer Copeland warns against preachers attempting to disguise themselves as a generic human being: Copeland, *Feminine Registers: The Importance of Women's Voices for Christian Preaching*. Eugene, OR: Cascade, 2014, p. 73.

34 This is an important point which is explored in David Buttrick, 1987, *Homiletic: Moves and Structures*, Philadelphia: Fortress, pp. 421–2.

35 Greek translation sourced from https://biblehub.com/multilingual/matthew/1-1.htm accessed 3.5.21.

36 Matthew 3.15.

37 Matthew 3.17.

38 Matthew 13.3, 13.31 and 13.44.

39 Matthew 11.12.

40 Matthew 5.3, 19.14 and 5.10.

41 Matthew 5.6, 5.10 and 6.33.

6

Present Preaching: A Conclusion Leading to Practice

To the present preacher

Concluding a book is rather like taking a baby into the world for the first time. The parent believes it is beautiful. The parent remembers the sweat and tears and joys of producing it. Just a little bit of parental protection would prefer to keep the baby at home a while longer. But it is time to conclude, to carry this baby into the world, and begin to wonder how it will be received.

Part of us wants our work to be loved. But as preachers, we recognize that is probably the least effective means of making a difference. We pray that what you have read here will provoke you to thought and action, to exploring the Now Homiletic, in which the preacher is recognizably there in the sermon. Recognized by themselves as clay jars that shape the treasure within and determine how it is poured out. Recognized by the congregation as people of integrity, faith, and hope. Recognized by God too, as of God, before God speaking in Christ.

> You are in your preaching. Your God-given role is to occupy that space as one who has been present to the text, is now present to the hearers and strives always to be present to the One who is ever old and ever new. This is less about what we present and more about being present. This is always personal, and it is always now.

This is the Now Homiletic.

Back to practice

This chapter is different from those that precede it. Here we offer some examples of present preaching. These are talks that were written for pre-recorded services or for preaching live whether in person or not. They are real sermons from real preachers, who preach in their own voice in ways suited to their contexts. We have deliberately asked preachers who approach the task in different ways. In each example there are things that stimulate thoughts and questions about what it means to be present in our preaching. There are limits to the ways in which we can experience preaching from flat script, but we encourage you to accept as a gift from other preachers the examples that follow. At the end of the chapter are some questions, some general, some specific. We encourage you to engage with them, individually or with others, as a way of developing your preaching.

Preacher: Jenny Bridgman, Director of Studies for Pastoral Workers in the Diocese of Chester
Text: Luke 2.22–38; Blood, mess and tears: A Candlemas song
Context: Parish service on social media

The following sermon was preached via video-link for Candlemas 2021. It is the result of many years of me inhabiting Mary's story through my own experiences, and it was formed over time into an autobiographical encounter with this part of Scripture. Since I preached this, national events have further heightened my awareness of the silencing of women in my own society: clearly, we have much to do if we are to give voice to one another.

Her silence screams through this story. Voiceless amid the raging hormones, she presents herself and her child: vulnerable but strong; polluted by blood destined to make others pure. This is her story, told by men, through men, for men.

This is Candlemas. A scene unfolding around the healing body of a woman who would have been torn open in childbirth, and who was about to hear the terrifying prophecy of a sword piercing her soul at the pain she would watch her son encounter as he grew.

We are sheltered from the gritty, earthy, fleshy, feminine parts of this story. Mary's voice is silenced as her story is told through the song of a man.

Forty days marked Mary's moment of purification. Forty days postnatal is an important milestone for any mother and baby: the wounds inflicted by birth will be knitting together again; there will be signs that the baby is gaining weight; rest may be less elusive as the baby sleeps for longer stretches; breastfeeding should be more comfortable; bottle feeding easier to anticipate and plan; the baby may have started to smile and make eye contact.

In the UK, women who have had a baby have a check-up after six weeks for these reasons. It's the 'magic' moment, where life may take on a semblance of normality once more. But oh-so-slowly: a new mum at six weeks postnatal will still feel vulnerable, wobbly and sore.

How did Mary feel, as she stood in a world of men in this most female of moments? Was her baby sleeping well? Was he thriving and gaining weight? Were her nipples cracked and sore? Had her vaginal trauma healed? Was she still riddled with the hormone-induced anxiety that kept her constantly watchful of this fragile life? Was she obsessed with protecting her son with a fierce love that burned in every ounce of her being?

I was in the throes of new motherhood when I first discovered Bellini's painting of the Presentation at the Temple. Fourteen centuries after this scene unfolded, Bellini begins to give Mary a voice. Luke doesn't tell us how Mary felt as she embarked on motherhood. How much did this vulnerable, sleep-deprived girl sweat or hold back tears as she handed her baby over to Simeon? How much did her heart plummet as Simeon spoke of a piercing sword?

Luke says only that she was amazed. How much did her amazement overwhelm her? Thrill her? Frighten her? What would she have said, using her own words, if she had been given a voice to tell this story?

Bellini tells us what Luke does not. Here is young courageous Mary, flanked by women, hesitating as she passes her tiny bundle to Simeon. The world of women faces off against the world of men, as the Christ child passes between them.

What is that hesitation? Is Mary beginning to understand the fullness of her vocation and the pain that it will cause her? Is she, like any new mother, finding it hard to trust a stranger with the wellbeing of her child, even for a moment?

Bellini paints the vulnerability and courage of every new mother. In Mary's eyes I see the turmoil of my own postnatal storm: the anxiety, the exhaustion, the depression, the joy, the fear, the pain. Bellini gives Mary the voice denied her by Luke, by Simeon, by the men who surround this scene so central to her role as God Bearer.

There is a multitude of people among us denied a voice. The light of revelation is blocked by shadows of oppression: a darkness that falls across people and nations to keep them hidden and unheard. And yet, there is hope in the modern-day Bellinis who are recasting the light to shine into the shadows as they paint scenes unseen. In vulnerability and with great courage, those denied a voice are nevertheless beginning to be heard.

I revisited my reflections on Bellini some years after first seeing his painting, the same day that Amanda Gorman, the USA's National Youth Poet Laureate and the youngest poet ever to read at a presidential inauguration was thrown into the media spotlight around the world, at the inauguration of Joe Biden as president of the United States. At the age of 22, this young black lady stood in a place where no one of her race, gender and age had previously been made welcome. And she took her moment and gifted the world with her courage, her vibrance and her joy.

And so what better challenge for us to hear again, on this Feast of Candlemas, than that offered by Amanda in her inauguration poem, 'The Hill We Climb': 'There is always light. If only we are brave enough to see it. If only we are brave enough to be it.'

I doubt Mary was silent that day. But through the centuries since she has rarely been given a voice. One of the most prominent figures of the Christian faith, she is also perhaps one of the most idolized, silenced and mistranslated. Dehumanized in her veneration; stripped of all that joins her with the experience of bringing life into the world: the blood, the mess, the tears – the very stuff of the Incarnation.

Seeing the light; being the light: these things are not just about who we are, what we say and do. They are about who we give a voice to. Who stands among us, gagged from telling their own story? Bringing light into the darkness of this world means making space for the silenced. If Simeon's song is to be enacted in all its fullness, then the voices of the silenced must be not only heard, but amplified.

Candlemas becomes not just a festival of light, but of song. Rich, harmonized melodies both on and off beat, as thousands join their voices to Simeon, to Mary, and sing their own stories in their own words. Purification becomes liberation. Peace becomes freedom. Salvation becomes song: the fullness of human experience shared as we who have a voice give way to the voiceless.

Preacher: Rich Wyld, Director of Portsmouth Pathway
Text: Mark 1.4–11
Context: Visiting preacher

In our Gospel reading today, from the first chapter of Mark, we hear about the baptism of Jesus and the baptism that John gives to Jesus and to so many people. There's this kind of a characteristic, straightforwardness with Mark who tells us that John 'appeared in the desert' or John was 'out in the desert', preaching a baptism of repentance for the forgiveness of sins. And when I read that word 'appeared' there in the NRSV I like to imagine that John just suddenly came out of nowhere. And of course that's not really what it means, but there is something really significant in that word, in the sense that John doesn't go into the city to get a big band of followers and then take them out into the desert, like a sort of monastic community. There's a sense in which John starts in the desert and people are going to him to hear his message.

In the church today, when we speak about our ministry and mission of proclaiming the gospel, we will often talk about going to where people are. That we've got a message that people need to hear, so we've got to go to where they are so that they can engage and hopefully respond. And of course, that's right and good. We see that in the Bible; we see Jesus doing just that.

It's striking to me that right at the beginning of Mark's gospel, John does the exact opposite. He does the exact wrong thing in terms of proclaiming his message. He's got a message to share with people, but he goes to the wilderness, the desolate place, the exact place where people *aren't* to proclaim his message. And gradually perhaps travelling, passing by, they hear what he has to say. And then they get to their destination and they pass it on and others come and hear, people are starting to choose to go out into the wilderness, to hear his message and respond. And more than that, his message is not just a message of comfort. It's not because people necessarily hear him saying what they want to hear. It's actually also a message of repentance. There's a challenge in that message.

So, he's not where the people are at. And what he's saying isn't necessarily what we might think they want to hear. And yet the people respond. People go out to hear what he has to say, to hear his challenge. It seems to me that there's something really important for us in that counter-intuitive image that we have here of John. It's not that we should not do what Jesus does in going to where people are. That's really important and right. But John, I think, reminds us of a couple of things: first, that within the Gospel message, within Jesus' message, there is a challenge. There's an uncomfortable element to it, but that's a really important thing that we must not lose sight of if we are to proclaim the gospel faithfully and if we're to hear it for ourselves. But perhaps also what John shows us and reminds us is that the remarkable thing is that people want that, actually people are up for the challenge. They're up for engaging with that more difficult message. They're tired of the insipid spirituality or a very busy kind of religion that gives them lots of things to do, but doesn't touch the deeper parts of their life, their existence. John's message is hard, but it speaks to the deepest, perhaps darkest depths of our human existence. It speaks to the fullness of life in all its complexity and pain and offers a message that brings hope to all, hope that speaks into our deepest reality. People are up for that. It's so significant. It's so potentially transformative that people are up for going out into the wilderness and they want to step into the unknown because they want something new, something transformative, something life-changing. So John offers a message, I think, that is challenging, but reminds us of the value and the power of that challenge to transform.

Also we remember then that John's message is not simply just about the repentance and the confession of sins, though that's a crucial part of it. It's not just that people are going out into the desert, to say how bad they are and to feel bad about themselves. This is not about the challenge just for its own sake. The challenge in part is because they actually step out into the unknown and as they reckon with the deepest realities of life, they find God in that and God meets them transformatively through Jesus Christ and through the gift of the Holy Spirit. What they're hearing is a message of hope in darkness, not ignoring the darkness on the one hand and not just saying that there's nothing to be said, but rather meeting God in that place and seeing the new world that God is bringing in Jesus. John says that Jesus is coming after him. And that just as John has baptized in water, a symbol that in a sense foreshadows, the way or foretells the way in which Jesus will baptize in the Holy Spirit. One of the things that often strikes me in that phrase is that it is not quite the image that we might think it is.

We often talk about the gift of the Holy Spirit dwelling inside us, that we receive the gift of the Spirit and the Spirit fills us and empowers us. And again, that's not wrong. That's right. That's a very biblical way of thinking. But the image here is sort of the other way around. John baptizes people in water – that word 'baptism' literally means 'dipping'. And so people are dipped in the water, immersed in the water. They go into the water, the water doesn't go into them unless they open their mouth at the wrong moment! And so, the image is the same here with the Holy

Spirit. To be baptized in the Spirit is not so much an image about the Spirit coming into us, but about us being immersed in the Holy Spirit – it's not either/or, in the Bible, it's both, both those images. But I think it's quite important just to note that in this situation, because if we only speak about the Holy Spirit coming into us, then there's a sense in which we can be left with the idea that the Spirit is this sort of thing that we need, we have and that we kind of carry around with us and it helps us out where we go and that is true. But if we only think of it in that way, you can always end up imagining, I still set the agenda for the day. I go, where I want to go, I do what I do, and the Spirit goes with me. And that's right, but there's another way of thinking about it here. Rather than the Spirit coming into us and then following our lead, in a sense to be immersed in the Spirit is to enter into the Holy Spirit's world and to be drawn into the life of the Spirit so that we follow together where the Spirit leads. There's that sense of a people being drawn into the life of the Holy Spirit as a community. It's the Holy Spirit that chooses where to go, it's the Holy Spirit that sets the agenda and that we're caught up in that movement, to follow faithfully, wherever the Spirit leads.

It's the sense that fits the symbol of going into the desert, where we step out of our comfort zone, our own sense of doing what we think we want to do, and trust in God. As we follow where the Spirit leaves, God leads us into a good place, not necessarily a comfortable place, that's important, but a place that's transformative. That's seeing the world renewed as God has intended it to be. That, I think, connects with the idea of Jesus himself receiving John's baptism, which always has sense of mystery about it that Mark doesn't resolve for us. Jesus accepts baptism. And of course, it's not that Jesus is confessing sin, Jesus goes without sin. So he doesn't need baptism in quite the same way. But I think what Jesus does do in that baptism he does in solidarity with us to show the way of stepping out in pure faith in God, in being immersed in the Holy Spirit to be fully faithful to God. He says, though, Jesus is kind of saying: 'this is the way this is the way to go'. He's joining us in that stepping out. He's leading us in that stepping out in faith that we might trust God wholly. It's not a comfortable thing to trust God. We like to be able to order our world neatly, but it's the most life-changing and profoundly beautiful thing to be able step out to say, actually, God, we will go where you go.

My prayer at the start of this troubled time, this troubled year where we're sort of in a kind of enforced wilderness of our own almost, is not so much that things would go back to the way they were. Although in a way, we do hope that. We certainly hope and pray that the vaccine will be delivered and that people will be well. But there is a real sense in which life will be different going on from here even once the pandemic is past – that we're not the same as we were. And my prayer is simply to recognize that in fact, life is always, really like that, if we notice it, there's always that sense that we are uncertain. There's that sense in the church, that things are changing, that the church is not going to be the way it used to be. And that might be a scary thing.

The crucial thing is that whatever we face, that we may open ourselves to the Spirit to be immersed in God's Spirit, to trust in God's Spirit, to lead us through those times of uncertainty and through, into the kingdom of God where we might see transformation and hope. So my prayer for us today that we would reopen ourselves to be renewed by God's Spirit. And that whatever happens in this year ahead of us, we will be able to trust God, and step out into the unknown, but doing so knowing that God is faithful and good, and that God has renewed the world in Jesus Christ, brought us the forgiveness of sins and the hope of new life. And that as we step forward with him, we would know that together.

Amen.

With Rich's kind permission, this talk has been included to illustrate how we can preach good sermons yet miss the opportunity to be present as preachers. What is particularly interesting in this case is that Rich deliberately chose not to share any personal story in this talk. Writing after the sermon he offers the following explanation:

There's a bit of irony about the sense of presence in this sermon. I suspect the idea about John the Baptist's almost deliberate attempt not to meet people where they're at echoes a bit of my suspicion about how I interpret my own experience. Through life's ups and downs, I can feel quite uncertain about where God is in all of it, and worry that it's too easy to project God onto feeling a certain way about something. So, I like the idea of being drawn into a perspective beyond my own experience, where the presence and promise of God doesn't depend on how I experience it, how I feel, and so on. I can see that a lot of myself is reflected in the ideas of going into the wilderness, of being immersed in the life of Spirit rather than the Spirit entering into my life. The irony comes from almost not wanting to speak about my experience precisely because of my own experience. What I would want to think about for the future is how to communicate those ideas in a nonetheless appropriately present way.

Preacher: Simon Moore, Team Rector, Sutton Parish, St Helens, Lancashire
Text: Luke 12.13–34
Context: Lockdown Harvest Service

I begin with echoes of Frank Sinatra's perhaps most famous song, 'My Way' (do not worry I won't be singing it, just yet). If you were to count the number of times in verses 17–19 Luke records this parable of Jesus saying, 'I', 'my', or 'myself', you'll find that there are ten occasions when this rich individual uses such terminology. In fact, the list reads as: I, I, my, I'll, I, my, I, my, I'll, myself.

It's something of a journey, an alliteration of self-centredness. This is all about me. It's all about me, eyeing up the biggest slice of the cake. Things that I have personally struggled with. Wanting to be in control, thinking that I know best, a worrying arrogance of self-preservation. It's fairly obvious that this rich fool has been involved in them as well.

It's a tragic story of a rich man with an abundant harvest. He imagined that the wealth he had was his, and he could do what he liked with it. He did what he liked with it in life, and there wouldn't be any consequence. The tragedy, of course, is – and the foolishness was – that he was generous to only himself.

Why? Why was this the case? Well, I guess, if we're honest, all of us from time to time have an inner desire to minimize the worry and fear about the future.

The context of chapter 12 is such that Jesus is addressing priorities in life and pointing very specifically that greed destroys. The barns of this rich fool are a testimony to empire building, an empire built on arrogance. Now, there's nothing wrong with wealth, but it's what we do with it. It's how much we keep for ourselves, it's how much we bless others with it. Wealth is a tool, what do we build and mend with it and who for? The harvest reminds us that it is God who provides, because all the meteorological and soil and crop conditions were the things that God had provided in the first place.

Of course, as God provides, what can we provide in responding to others ourselves? Boy, are we good at justifying our needs before others! Surely, richness isn't a number. It's not an amount, but it's how generous we are to others. It reminds us of that echo of the widow's mite who gave all. We have a God who gave all, nailed to the cross of history.

Now, at the time of this sermon the richest man in the world was Jeff Bezos. He has just been overtaken by Elon Musk. But at the time of the sermon, he was worth about $181 billion, roughly £140 billion.

Now, just to put that in some sort of sense. If Bezos is worth $181 billion, the World Health Organization have worked out that just over $11 billion would give the world clean drinking water. You could save the Amazon rainforest for $64 billion. He did give away $2 billion in 2018. It's too easy, isn't it though to lose focus when we concern ourselves with what Jeff Bezos and others who are mega rich are doing with their wealth. But we forget to think about it for ourselves, because we do worry and feel we need to make ourselves secure. Like the foolish farmer, we want to have some level of security and control. We want to keep the doors of our barns of resources under lock and key, and it is our lock and our key! Whose harvest is it?

The reality is, we will never have enough. We'll never fully be satisfied. When the early lottery winners in the UK were being interviewed, there were two things they all said, and remember they had already won at least a £1m. They said they'd wish that they'd won more, and they had wished that they'd won it earlier. There's no doubt that these store houses, these barns of resources, time, treasure and talent can become a barrier between us and others and God, rather than a tool we wield for him to bless others.

So, on this Harvest Sunday, there's a very profound question: who is the Lord of the Harvest? Jesus goes on to use pictures of provisions of birds and flowers. There is that wonderful maxim, how much more does your Father in heaven care for you? How much more does our father in heaven bless us? Look what he does with nature and creation. Do you think he's not going to care for you and me?

John Wyatt writing in *Christianity Magazine* talked about hope. He mentioned that we cannot change the past, it's already happened. We certainly can't predict the future. Tim Keller once said that worriers are visionaries without the optimism. But we can change our thinking and responses for the present. The tragedy of the rich fool was that he was living in the future and not in the present, not considering what he could do with this abundance of harvest.

But it is a good time to worry. There are good reasons to worry now amid a pandemic that is driving so much hurt and uncertainty and pain. Just in the areas of mental health, there's increasing situations of phobias, panic buying, TV binge-watching, excessive alcohol intake, use of phone helplines, self-harm, abuse and depression. Coupled with that: job loss, economic uncertainty, disrupted education ...

But constant worry is debilitating. It diminishes us. It breaks us down, and it makes us look for security and safety in things, and not in God. Having said that, being fearful can save us. Just recently, Kyle Burgess was out running in Utah Slate Canyon when he encountered a mountain lion on his ten-mile run, who did not take very kindly to him, and followed him for six minutes as he videoed it live (catch it on YouTube), wondering whether his life was going to come to an end. His fear drove him to action and safety, ultimately.

As followers of Jesus, there are probably at least two equal dangers wrestling within us. One, we can presume that God's going to give us comprehensive life insurance, or, two, despair that there is no hope. We're not immune from the storms of life, but we can have confidence because there is hope. God brings and points us to a heavenly security. Despite the earthly uncertainty of each day, He deals in hope and eternity. The rich fool was pursuing earthly security, despite the ongoing nature of earthly uncertainty. Fear is driving his actions, and it's temporary and ephemeral, and it comes tragically to an end for him.

The psalmist in Psalm 56.3 writes, 'When I am afraid, I put my trust in you', and that's our invitation to remember God's provision as we look back on our lives, to remind ourselves that goodness and love will follow us, will follow me all the days of my life. Hindsight is a wonderful thing, but I stand here today as I recall the chapters of my life where this is true ... exhausted and abseiling down Mount Kenya in the dark; anguished prayers and then safety after eighteen abseils. Wondering how we were going to pay our Bible college fees to find anonymous envelopes with cash in our pigeonhole.

In Psalm 23, I remember God's presence now. God is with us even in the valley of the shadow of death. Earlier this year I haemorrhaged after a routine operation which went terribly wrong, light now, dark then, but God ever present.

We are all so palpably there right now, in the shadows, in this present climate of a world pandemic.

Yet, we can hold on to God's promises for the future that he is with us. 'I am with you always, to the end of the age,' we read in Matthew 28.20. Sometimes we ask: 'What next?' to discover that we will experience more of the same until otherwise directed, yet we do this with the freedom that comes from knowing God as a daily guide and companion.

We are invited as a result of all the things that God brings to us and blesses us with, to make our part of the harvest a blessing for others, to combat injustice and inequality in the world. So, how might you and I use our share right now? I could come up with a list, but that's my list. It's not yours.

So, we're going to pray now together that God will inspire and guide and challenge you and I to respond to what we might do, to bless others with God's harvest, and to bring people into a knowledge of His eternal and saving love. In Christ, let us pray.

Simon offered some interesting background information about this talk. He writes:

Intriguingly as I reviewed the first draft of this sermon and preached it to myself, I found it lacked my fingerprint, elements of myself. To be present to the congregation, I had to ask: 'How has this been true for me over the years?' I had to go back and redraft a personal response to the psalm's invitation so that I might own their promises and provision. I try to remember that I am preaching to others and myself. A lack of personal engagement in a sermon can create a concern about the integrity of the preacher. The hearers may well ask: 'is this preacher with us in this?'

Another feature of this talk is Simon's approach to encouraging a response. He writes:

I've increasingly tried to avoid being directive. I don't find the tick list of possible applications to live out the sermon a helpful approach. I think that this can often reflect a church's vision agenda rather than God's! I try to give space at the end of a sermon to listen silently to God in prayer. This invites hearers to be present to God and hear confirmation, personal conviction, or whatever is part of God's call and invitation to them.

Preacher: Grace Thomas, Priest in Moss Side and Whalley Range and Diocesan Environment Officer, Manchester
Text: Psalm 24, Creationtide
Context: On Zoom to an ecumenical church in the city centre.

I had visited the church once, before the pandemic, and knew it to be a diverse congregation in terms of age and ethnicity. I was given free rein regarding readings and so decided to focus on Psalm 24 and draw some themes out that would relate to the season of Creationtide, within which this service fell.

Sermon – The Earth is the Lord's

The earth is the LORD's and all that is in it, the world, and those who live in it; for he has founded it on the seas, and established it on the rivers.
Who remembers what we heard in the skies during spring? I remember. I remember people talking in awe and wonder about it. It happens every year, yet, somehow, in a time of such grief and upheaval, our senses were directed to the chorus of the birds in a way they hadn't been for a while. Had we simply spent the past years not noticing? Was it because the streets were suddenly so much quieter? Whatever the reason, the songs were a welcome gift. And a gift not of our making at all.

Who shall ascend the hill of the LORD? And who shall stand in his holy place?
Walter Brueggemann, in a study of Psalm 24, directs us to remember who really owns the land upon which we live.[1] Land ownership – who has the right to the land, who belongs in the land, who can rule over the land – are questions that have been a part of human history. As Brueggemann points out, when we humans declare ownership of land, it is nearly always primarily out of a sense of self-interest and gain, rather than responsibility and gratitude towards creation. Historically, land has been claimed time and time again in the name of 'progression' and need, without much consideration for the land itself, or recogni-

tion over its worth beyond what we have wanted from it. From the fifteenth century onwards, colonial powers grabbed land for their own benefit. Land which holds resources perceived as vital for advancement, such as fuel, minerals, space for farming, is being seized and fought over.

Pride in progression is a stalwart feature of contemporary Western society. We celebrate our technological achievements and how far we have developed in so many ways. There is much to celebrate. Indeed, we are able to join in worship today because of advances that can bring us together online. Yet the idol of progression can only take us so far.

Those who have clean hands and pure hearts, who do not lift up their souls to what is false, and do not swear deceitfully. They will receive blessing from the Lord.

In claiming the land in the way we have, we have all too often taken credit for what it produces. As if all of this is of our achievement. Viewing something as 'ours' often leads to us viewing all that comes from it as 'ours' and of our making, too. The world is viewed through our anthropocentric – that is, human centred – lens. Recently, someone, talking to me about the climate emergency, started by saying 'I don't like the phrase "saving the world".' I nodded in keen agreement, thinking the conversation was going in the direction of examining who 'saves'. However, my companion followed up his statement by saying 'It's about saving humanity, isn't it?'

We can so often view creation through the lens of our own importance. Land belongs to us. We are advancing, developing, improving, enhancing. There's a real danger in positioning ourselves in this way, as we can witness in the ecological breakdowns that are increasing in number. Does it also impact on how we relate to creation? What we notice? What we skip by? The Psalmist reminds us that not only is the land the Lord's, but everything that is in it, the world all those who live in it. The birdsong, the flowers, these things that have lifted us in difficult times, are part of something more vast and magnificent than anything we could ever achieve, no matter how much land we claim as our own, or how advanced we are.

Even in an urban context, where human concrete, metal and glass creations dominate the landscape, the natural world is never too far away. Plants pierce the tarmac. Trees stand proudly by the roadside. I tentatively took up cycling in the lockdown. As I journeyed through the city, I noticed these things in a way I hadn't before. It will be harvest in a few weeks and at my home church, we will probably sing that old favourite 'We plough the fields and scatter', because even in the city the harvest of creation is abundant. On the curry mile, spiced aromas fill the air as people knead naan dough, and stir fry – the good food from the land. In the alleyways of Moss Side, green spaces have been curated by residents among the cobbles. Terracotta pots spill over with vibrant colours of flowers that have been fed and watered by God's almighty hand. While we live on the land, and take the fruits of the land to enjoy and benefit from, none of this, ultimately, is of our doing. So much of it goes unnoticed.

Who is the King of glory? The LORD, strong and mighty.
God reminds us throughout scripture that it is at the hands of the divine that the created world came to be. The poem of Genesis 1 sets out how God created everything, and declared is all 'very good'.[2] In the book of Job, God asks 'Have you commanded the morning since your days began, and caused the dawn to know its place …? Is it by your wisdom that the hawk soars …? Is it at your command that the eagle mounts up …?'[3] As advanced as we are, we stand in awe of a Creator whose ownership of the land is ultimate, and whose tending, cherishing and renewing of the very good creation, of which we are a part, brings us hope and solace in a way none of our advances ever could do.

Nothing I am telling you is anything new. Yet, maybe there is wisdom in remembering how we were so taken by the songs and colours of spring this year. Had we, somehow, not been previously as attuned to the gifts of creation as we could have been, and only took notice when so much of our lives were dramatically curtailed? Has the anthropocentric culture in which we are steeped distracted us from stopping and noticing the magnificence of creation – carried as we are on crest of human success and acquisition? Brueggemann suggests that the preacher, when looking at Psalm 24, is placed as a witness and advocate for land as creation in a society that is ideologically committed to land as possession.[4] I don't know I can articulate it as well as Brueggemann would desire, but I'm not sure I need to. I think what I need to do is to simply encourage us all to not lose the focus we gained in spring, but to learn from it, and attend to what it means.

Who is this King of glory? The LORD of hosts, he is the King of glory.
We inhabit a land of divine creation, surrounded by delights, large and small. This Creationtide is a perfect time to remember whose land this is and give thanks.

The Earth is the Lord's and all that is in it. The world, and those who live in it.

And what a world it is.

Amen.

Preacher: Kate Bruce, Chaplain at RAF Brize Norton in Oxfordshire
Text: Ephesians 2.1–10
Context: Zoom, guest speaker

I wanted to draw on my own grotty mood, how the scripture spoke into that and opened some windows on what God is saying now – by way of encouraging my hearers, and myself! I knew two of the congregation. The rest were strangers to me.

Sermon – Freedom from the locked-down life

I don't know about you, but I am heartily sick of the present moment. I don't like working from home. I don't like being on my own for endless days. I want to be around people. I'm lonely and fed up. I feel some days like I am living a one-dimensional existence in black and white and I want some colour. I want freedom from the locked down life and I want it now.

If that whinge resonates with you, our reading from Ephesians 2 offers some rich blessing and plenty of colour, and a reminder that we are free from the ultimate lockdown. Hold that thought.

In the Harry Potter books, two dimensions are seen to co-exist at the same time. Muggles are only aware of the ordinary everyday, but the wizarding world experiences another dimension running alongside the muggle world, a deeper reality beyond the way things seem. It's a picture that sprang to mind as I pondered the reading from Ephesians – which speaks of realities within and beyond the ordinary everyday.

Paul describes how there was a point at which his readers were spiritually dead, unaware of God and the dimensions of God's love and life. They were in a spiritual state of lockdown, spiritual Muggles, but now they are free, aware of a deeper reality within and beyond the immediate. They are moving 'further up and further in', to borrow the language of Narnia. We might be in physical lockdown just now, but like the Ephesians we don't have to be in spiritual lockdown.

The state of spiritual death Paul refers to is a life enslaved to the drive of the self, a life lived in black and white, based on acquisition of stuff and the satisfaction of immediate hungers and drives. It's a life that is one-dimensional, lived in muted shades, focused on the here and now and nothing more. But God offers colour – a multi-dimensional life which is intense in love, full of possibility, a life of rich desire for God. Without God we remain locked down in single-dimensional living, unable to perceive the divine world right under our noses. Doomed to blunder along in muted shades. But because God is 'rich in mercy' – he breaks the chains that enslave us to our blinkered, grasping drive for self-fulfilment. God says 'leave the chains behind and come.' No more lockdown.

Paul reminds the Ephesians that once they were enslaved to 'the ruler of the power of the air.' It's a strange expression – linked to disobedience. It seems odd language until we ask ourselves where we see the fruit of this enslavement. Then it all becomes crystal clear.

- When the spirit of 'I'm all right Jack' is at work – leading to a vaccine grab, or stockpiling loo rolls and resources – the ruler of the power of the air is being worshipped.
- Where children are used and abused with impunity, where the voices of survivors are pushed out to protect the perpetrators – we are in the realm of disobedience, where passions of the flesh will bring the wrath of God.
- Where vulnerable people are manipulated to satisfy the desires of the powerful – you can be sure people are living in one dimension, where love, mercy and judgement are not seen, or else disregarded, labelled as fake news. When we see this, or peddle it, be sure this ruler is rubbing hands with glee.

'The ruler of the power of the air' might seem an odd expression – but it is not difficult to see when and where the evil that locks down is abroad.

'Not so with you', says Paul, implicitly. 'You once lived as though anything goes. Not any more.' To live in colour is to see sin clearly – and be aware and honest about our own failings and open to the rich possibilities of life with God. God draws us into a life of colour, richness, possibility, and community together in Christ Jesus. In spite of being stuck at home, this is life with no lockdown.

God opens our eyes to the reality amidst and beyond this present moment. God gathers us into the life of Jesus. This is a life which is not limited by the locked down boundaries of our humanity. It draws us up into richer possibility and deeper perspective.

An example. Last week I was at the funeral of a friend and colleague, Dr Bex Lewis, who died of cancer at 45. Outside the church I met a friend and we raged together in language which might be regarded as a tad unbecoming. Perhaps, but it was honest. Seeing her coffin brought into church looked like the final and ultimate lockdown. Death. The funeral address, delivered with such integrity and gentle conviction (thanks Andrew Graystone) was brilliant because it was honest about the outrage of this death, of the profound hurt and loss, of life cut short.

But we were reminded that there is always more with God. Not with a 'there, there', soft soap kind of hope, that mutes the agony of grief, but with the promise that in the midst of death God is always at work doing a new thing, working in dimensions we cannot yet really grasp. The fact that we can only gain a hint, an intimation of this future freedom does not mean it is unreal. God unbolts the locks of death.

God is always calling us further up and further into this life of promise and purpose – blessed by kindness and love, marked by generosity. It is all gift – this fulness of life. There is no room for boasting or pride. We cannot earn this life by chalking up good deeds – it is given and received as gift – and out of this gratitude flows, expressed in acts of kindness and love. This is the way of life of the community of God; good deeds as an expression of love received, not a bartering tool to deserve love.

This way of seeing requires deliberate openness to God, a daily co-operation with God's invitation to step into this perception of life in all its fulness. It asks us to be present to God. Sometimes I find myself all too readily present to my struggles and stresses. I sense God challenge me with a wry smile – 'If you'd just look to me a little more often in your day, Kate, and chewed on your troubles a little less – you'd find more security in the freedom I'm calling you into.'

The one who is locked down in spiritual Muggledom, trapped in trespass and sin, is like a person who, on a day when the sun shines brightly in a clear blue sky, draws the curtains and hunkers down before a two-bar electric fire, feeling smug about how well they are keeping themselves warm.

Not so with you. You heard the call of divine love and have thrown back the curtains and stepped into light. You are made alive in Christ by the rich mercy of God. Raised up from the grave of sin and destined for things beyond imagining.

Who wants a life locked up in the shadows when God calls us into a life of light and love, generosity and gift? Hope and wild possibility.

The natural world gives us intimations of this in the yearly rhythm of new life, the unlikely boring up of the snowdrop through the icy earth, the irrepressible dancing daffodils, the splashes of colour of the wayside crocus. We are not made to live in winter, in black and white and shades of grey. We are not meant for lockdown – spiritual or actual. We are made for life in freedom and rich colour.

But, we might say.

But ... this is a letter to the Ephesians. I'm not an Ephesian. It's all very rich and wonderful – but does it apply to me, now, today? Me, in my fear and fragility. Me, in my weakness and uncertainty? Me in my grumpiness, sadness, loneliness?

To any who feel the drag of sin and failure – fear not. Draw close to the God who draws close to you. Say your truth and trust God's forgiveness and help. Watch the chains fall off.

To any who have known the lockdown blues and the creeping nausea of despair – it's ok. You are known and understood. Come close to the God who is already close to you. Hear the bolts slide back.

To any who feel not good enough – it was never about you being able to earn God's love – it is all gift. Come near with open arms to the one whose arms are open for you. Feel your heart unlock

To any who worry about finance, health, family, the environment, whether covid will ever end – do not let fear prevent you from hearing God's call to you. Whatever you face, you can face it with the God of resurrection power. See the stone rolled back.

I began having a whinge about lockdown – which is fair enough, I think. But let's not get stuck there. I end with this thought. One day, this season will end and we will walk out and meet and mingle – and be overjoyed. Can we catch that joy now by perceiving another dimension alongside this world of physical restriction? God frees us from the lockdowns of sin and failure and despair and loneliness and grief, and alienation and ultimately the lockdown of death.

Open the door of your heart,
Open the windows of your mind
Open the skylight of your imagination.

You are free.
Lockdown is over.
Come further up and further in.
Amen.

Preacher: Deirdre Brower Latz, Principal and Senior Lecturer, Nazarene Theological College, Manchester
Text: Isaiah 53; Romans 8.14–39; Hebrews 4.14–16; John 14
Context: Mixed congregation, college chapel

I suppose there are different ways into the ideas of lament and our faith-story. We could start with a plaintive question, in a dusky evening, with hushed voices and crouching bodies, hiding from God. The tender, anguished, hopeful, hurt question comes: 'Where are you? Why are you hiding? What have you done?' God's lament over broken people, their mistaken understanding and action twisting them away from Godself: And God's heart fractures a bit.

Or, perhaps, it's the blood pools on the ground that invites us into lament. The man killed, his body's blood staining earth – the murderer a brother – and the blood itself crying out: And God's heart fractures a bit.

Maybe we're invited into the whispering cry of oppressed people – backs aching under the burden of mud-clay packed bricks. A swelling whisper of pain, suffering, murmurings that wend their way to Gods' ear: And God's heart fractures a bit.

When we think about lament, as we tiptoe through Scriptures, I wonder about the lament of camps wiped out by swarms; first-born babies' still hands cradled in the palm of an Egyptian mother – breathing no more. The grief of it. I wonder about the grief of the families shredded by the red-sea closing over their loved ones as they chase the people of Israel. Lament.

I wonder about the lament of the broken body of a young woman dumped on the doorstep of her fathers' house, torn apart by gang rape in Judges 19. The lament rising: And God's heart fractures a bit.

I wonder about the lament of the courtiers, seeing their king unravelling – he'd seemed so blessed, but this man with spittled mouth, raving and raging against the usurping David, this great once-King, now a shadow of himself. Lament fracturing, rising, hurting, real ... The great now revealed as the weak: And God's heart fractures a bit.

I think of the lament of that same David, as his own destructive desires are revealed, and oppression, abuse, rape, violence, wrong-doing creeps into his own life. The lament of the prophet, the lament of God.

I think of the other voices who see valleys strewn with brittle bones, picked clean: these were people once – their death and their bones a deep sorrow. The lament of a prophet who sees widows starving, their large-bellied children too lethargic to wipe the flies from their eyes. Lament, lament, lament. And God's heart fractures a bit.

As we carry on leafing through our Book, we see the twisting of worship – the sacrifices and blood-stained altars a curse. The lament as the people use false scales and starve their neighbours. Or underpay them. The lament as twisted leaders cruelly suppress. As priestly leaders get fat and rich and their poor brothers and sisters in faith die, their bones heaped in pauper's graves. Lament. And God's heart fractures a bit.

When we realize that God is the original lamenter – God as in tender relationship with humankind that's marked by lament, is it any wonder that we get to hope only through 'A man of sorrows and acquainted with grief'?

The lament continues – overt, underlying, pain-filled, corporate, and personal.

Lament marks Jesus' birth, when innocents are slaughtered. Rachel's tears and mothers' tears mingling as Herod sweeps through and kills. Mary's tears soak swaddling.

Lament marks the tracks of tears on Jesus' face when he knows his friend's corpse is rotting three days away.

Lament marks the voice of Jesus, when he calls his rich young friend to a deeper way, a stronger path, a sacrificial life – and sees him walk away.

Lament marks Jesus' conversations, when he encounters women, on their knees in terror before the men who would kill them to justify their own hidden sins.

Lament marks Jesus, as he sees flesh eaten by leprosy, or the drained face of anaemia at the steady blood loss over decades.

Lament marks Jesus, when he says 'My friend' and is kissed in a garden. Lament. Lament. Lament. And God's heart fractures a bit.

Lament marks Jesus in prayer. 'If there's any other way.' Lament marks Jesus in wounds we call stripes. Lament.

And, God weeps. And the earth is split open with mingling of sorrow and love. And breath ends and death comes. And death ends and breath starts. And ... Resurrection!

But this is a sermon on lament. Lament. Lament.

When we lament, we enter into the space of the Holy. The Holy One of God knows the places of sorrow and grief. Knows the fracturing of pain and the horrors of loss. Knows the deepest places of pain, shock, suffering – inflicted, wounded, suffering.

Who laments? Our God. Sustainer, creator, lover of the universe.

Who laments? Christ, our Lord, our friend, our suffering saviour.

Who laments? The Spirit, who joins our groaning, and interprets our cries to the very ear of God.

Who laments? Father, Son and Spirit.

Who laments? We do.

When we join in Christ, we join one who knows the deepest places of our fears, of our fracturing, of our pain, of our lives. We join one who weeps.

Thank God for a weeping Jesus.

Thank God that the heart of God is sorrowing, questing, seeking, searching, present.

Thank God that the questions of lament are woven into the fabric of our faith:

Where are you?

Why are you hiding?

What have you done?

These questions, first on the heart of God are echoed by us, right?
Where are you, God?
Why are you hiding, God?
What have you done, God? (or not done, God?)

In these moments, we linger in lament, in these trigger areas of our lives, in these stories of trauma and suffering, in these places of pain and sorrow, we linger in lament of hates, of pains, of sufferings, of deaths, of doing the things we don't want to do, in saying the things we shouldn't say. We lament in the little places of our lives where our realities don't match our dreams. Where we've borne shame, not our own, where we've harmed in ways beyond us. We lament in the big places of our lives where the interruptions of such grief swell us beyond our capacity to bear. We lament in the silent places of our souls where we ran out of words, prayers ago. We lament at the death of the world, at the death of others, at our own death. We lament at the suffering world, no place untouched. We lament at the aching church, so imperfect. We lament at the reality and the possibility that pain doesn't end in the morning. Each day offering new moments of grief.

Who laments? We do.

We lament with gritted teeth. We lament with song. We lament in tears. We lament with others. We lament in our hearts. We lament with our lips. We are acquainted with grief. We lament, and if we listen closely, we hear our lamenting echoed, echoing. We lament in a holy concert. Our minor-key music of lament joining in the blues, the spirituals, the rhythm of the Psalms. Our songs of lament harpless, but melodic – riffing on God's songs of lament.

And, in the middle of our lament, if we breathe in, we discover that our grief and lament is a measure of our love, and of the heart of God.

In the middle of our pain, if we stop – when we pause – we realize that our lament's song is attuned to a deep truth: this isn't as it should be.

And, the lament we offer is a measure of the reality we *know* to be true: it isn't meant to be this way.

No – there's a deeper truth than even that – *It won't always be this way.*

Lament shapes our imagination. It works through us. But we can't get up too soon from the riverside weeping. Lament has to be sat with – because we're singing with God a love song of lament. If we lament in faith.

Lamenting in faith isn't just grief. It's not just sorrow. Lamenting is laced with love that is infused with the possibilities of life. Lament is on-our-knees-with-our-hands-open. Lament is *us* – together. Lament is here.

At the other side of our lament, comes the hope of peace. But we can't get there by a shortcut. The life we live in the now, is marked by the *hope* of the glory of the end. But we can't get there the easy way. If we could, no Gethsemane. No Judas. No Pilate. No Crucifixion. No death. We can't get to there, without the *here* of Lament.

Our lament is sprinkled with yeast of hope. Our lament is touched with saltiness, but that salt of hope comes from our tears. Our lament brings us the hope of peace. Yes. Of the restoration of the world. Of the loved ones with us at the banquet. Of the world in technicolour, vibrant with life. Pure waters flowing, babies at play, old folk wise, bones strong, breath easy, trees fruitful, fields abundant, sickness unheard of. All *yes*. All yes. A resurrection life!

But – to get to the other side of deepest lament, we have to go through the lament.

At the other side of lament, we *are* shaped into a new person, new people, a new creation, the tracks of our tears captured in God's bottle and salting the seas … But though the other side of lament is our hope and possibility, is the place of the centring of our peace, is the place of no more hiding, no more shame, no more plaintive cries … That's the other side. Here, now, it's lament.

Of course, the question for us is – what do we do with this? The litany of laments?

We sit.
We sit with it.
We pause.
We stop.

We become people with expansive hearts and the space to lament – hospitable to lament so that others can come to the riverside, sit with us and weep. And ... through that space of shared lament, find a way of joined-up-hope. The body ... the whole ... the hope ...

Ushered into weeping, knowing that the one who catches all tears, who wipes all tears, sits with us – and that in the morning ... at the dawn of the new day, in a garden, in a city, there will be a new story written, with new life swelling up, with hope's completion bringing joy. Joy after lament. Hope comes with the morning. Meanwhile, here, now: Nothing can separate us from the Love of God in Christ. God is with us. God is with you.

Questions for further reflection

God

- How often do your current or recent experiences of God feature in your preaching? In which of these sermons do you feel the preacher revealed this for themselves?
- Which of these preachers do you feel created space for people to encounter God? How do you do this?

Self

- Some of these sermons depend on personal experience to explore new ways into the biblical text. What significant experiences have you had that 'flavour' your preaching?
- Which of these sermons most closely matches how you preach? How might you take that sermon and develop it if you were preaching it now?

- Kate was aware of her own life stage and how it affected her preaching. How might you become more aware of your life stage and its impact on what you preach?

Bible

- Kate reads the Bible from amidst difficult circumstances. Deirdre explores difficult times in the Bible. How does present darkness feature in your preaching?

- Deirdre's sermon is longer than the others and is based on a biblical theme. How does your congregation's expectations about sermon length and content affect the ways in which you might be present as a preacher?

- What do you think about the way Jenny uses her personal experience to engage with the biblical text? What might you have brought to a reading of that passage?

Congregation

- One of the striking features of Grace's sermon is the sense of place within it. It demonstrates being present to a congregation by knowing where they live and breathing the local air. How does where your congregation live inform how you preach?

- Do you think it would have helped the hearers to better understand Rich's sermon if the explanation offered afterwards had been included in the talk itself or do you think it might have been a distraction?

- Is it possible to be present in a sermon without being explicitly present through personal story? If so, how?

- Look at Simon's sermon again. Would you have made any different choices in terms of the ending?

- Looking back at all the sermons in the book, in what ways do you think the preachers demonstrate that they are present and will leave the congregation with something which is for now?

Notes

1 W. Brueggemann, 2012, *Remember You Are Dust*, Eugene, OR: Cascade Books.
2 Genesis 1.31.
3 Job 38.12, 16; 39.26, 27.
4 Brueggemann, *Remember*, p. 69.

Afterword

THE RT REVD PHILIP NORTH

I am going to start by breaking the fourth wall. I don't really know what someone writing an afterword is meant to do. Should I be picking out the highlights from what we've just read? That would be a challenging task indeed from a book that, despite its brevity, contains more gleaming gems than a pirate's stash of treasure. Or am I meant to be adding to it with some fresh insight of my own? Since I find myself locked down by ignorance, I will try to do both.

I was tremendously relieved by Liz's assertion in Chapter 2 that the role of the preacher is not just to preach but to live 'a preaching life' because I have often wondered if my fascination with preaching borders on an unhealthy obsession. When my nephews and nieces were young I used to drive them mad by plundering every aspect of their lives for Gospel illustrations. The phrase, 'That'll preach' is one that often comes into my mind when faced with life's coincidences, contingencies and catastrophes. And I'm not alone. When I run preaching courses in the diocese, the participants also confess a preoccupation with preaching that can leave their friends thinking that they are unbalanced.

It was such a relief then for Liz to explain that a fascination with preaching is really a fascination with God; that the present preacher is above all present to God. Preaching is empty, hollow and hypocritical if it does not spring directly from lively relationship with the God we meet in Jesus Christ.

But the problem with saying something like that is that it can leave us feeling inadequate. What if we're weary? What if we're tired? What if we are going through one of those dark

AFTERWORD

patches in our lives when we need to rely on the faith and prayer of others? A risk with books and lectures about preaching is that they can all too easily leave us feeling unworthy of the task. And that's where I come to my addition.

Preaching invariably happens in the context of worship. In fact, preaching *is* worship. We don't pause the worship for a few minutes while the preacher struts their stuff and then pick up where we left off. Preaching is integral to the act of worship and so something which, while addressed to the people, is offered above all to God. In the Catholic tradition the priest who presides at the Mass will usually be the preacher to emphasize the unity of word and sacrament in a single act of worship.

And that actually should liberate us all the more to enjoy preaching in the way that this book encourages. The worship that we offer can never be perfect. The singing will be terrible. Or the projector will have broken down. Or the servers will be picking their noses. Or the priest will be late or ill-prepared. Or the churchwarden will have had a row with the flower arrangers. Or the person offering the prayers will have forgotten it's their turn on the rota. We should aim for quality in our worship, but perfection is a myth.

What makes our worship perfect is God. He transforms our weak and broken offerings and unites it with the ceaseless worship of heaven so that, from the midst of the mess, there is authentic encounter with the mind-blowing beauty of God.

And if that can be said of worship in general, it can most certainly be said of preaching. The present preacher must remember that the primary move comes from God who, in worship, makes himself present to them. Because if we remember that, we can delight in taking risks in our preaching, trusting in the work of our transforming God.

A story may illustrate the point. There was once a boy who, against his will, was taken to a concert to be given by a brilliant Russian maestro. The boy was furious about this enforced captivity, squashed into an uncomfortable stall in a packed and hot concert hall, and grew even more furious when the programme was delayed because of the tardiness of the performer. Eventually, filled with rebellious rage, the boy got up from his seat, clambered onto the podium, sat at the vast grand piano and began to play the only tune he knew. Which was 'Chopsticks'.

The audience were furious. 'Who is this child?' They asked. 'Throw him out! This is a disgrace!' But at that very moment the maestro himself appeared. He hushed the crowd with a gesture, walked up to the piano, gently put his arms either side of the boy, whispered 'keep playing' and began to improvise. And through his genius, the boy's dreadful music was transformed into something of breathtaking beauty such that the audience gasped.

Preachers should always aim for excellence. But we can also take delight in the fact that we will never achieve excellence, that no matter how hard we try we will never quite capture the essence of a passage, or communicate the fullness of the mystery of God, or answer exactly the questions that is on our listeners' hearts. We should delight in that, because that is the point where God takes over and works his transformation. For our preaching is worship and the ways in which it touches and changes the human heart are incomprehensible and indefinable.

So above all, enjoy preaching. Delight utterly in the incredible privilege of opening up the scriptures, communicating the wonder of God, capturing the imaginations of your hearers, bringing the ineffability of the divine into the mundane lives of ordinary people. Be yourself in your preaching rather than trying to ape the style and approach of others, no matter how lofty their reputation. Be creative, subversive, liberated in what you say. Do your very best.

But don't stress yourself out by aiming for perfection. For it is God who puts his arms around the shoulders of his preachers, who whispers to them 'Keep playing' and who transforms our frail efforts into something utterly beautiful to the glory of his name.

Bibliography

Allen, O. Wesley (ed.), *The Renewed Homiletic*, 2010, Minneapolis: Fortress Press.
Alter, R., 2007, *The Book of Psalms: A Translation with Commentary*. New York: W. W. Norton and Co.
Augustine, 2014, *Teaching Christianity: De Doctrina Christiana*, translated by Edmund Hill John E. Rotelle, Kindle Edition, Hyde Park: NY, New City Press.
Barth, Karl, 1991, *Homiletics*, Louisville, KY: Westminster John Knox.
Bass, Dorothy, 2016, 'Imagining: Biblical Imagination as a Dimension of Christian Practical Wisdom' in Dorothy C. Bass, Kathleen A. Cahalan, Bonnie J. Miller-McLemore, James R. Nieman and Christian Sharen (eds), *Christian Practical Wisdom: What it is, Why it Matters*, Grand Rapids: Eerdmans, pp. 232–74.
Beeke, Joel R., 2008, *Living for God's Glory: An Introduction to Calvinism*, Kindle Edition, Lake Mary, FL: Reformation Trust.
Briggs, Melody R., 2017, *How Children Read Biblical Narrative*. Eugene, OR: Wipf and Stock.
Bromiley, G. W., 'Karl Barth's Doctrine of Inspiration', *Journal of the Transactions of the Victoria Institute* 87 (1955), pp. 66–80.
Brown, B., 2010, *The Gifts of Imperfection*. Center City, Minnesota: Hazelden.
Brown, T., 2012, *Breaking the Fourth Wall: Direct Address in the Cinema*, Edinburgh: Edinburgh University Press.
Bruce, K., 2015, *Igniting the Heart: Preaching and Imagination*. London: SCM Press.
Bruce, Kate and Jamie Harrison (eds.), 2017, *Wrestling with the Word: Preaching Tricky Texts*, London: SPCK.
Brueggemann, W., 2012, *Remember You Are Dust*, Eugene, OR: Cascade.
Buttrick, David, 1987, *Homiletic: Moves and Structures*, Philadelphia: Fortress.
Cameron, H., "Life in all its Fullness' Engagement and Critique: Good News for Society' *Practical Theology* 5(1), (2012), pp. 11–26.
Copeland, J., 2014, *Feminine Registers: The Importance of Women's Voices for Christian Preaching*. Eugene, OR: Cascade.

Craddock, Fred, 1985, *Preaching*, Nashville, TN: Abingdon.
Craddock, Fred, 2001, *As One Without Authority*, 4th edn, St Louis, MO: Chalice.
Dunn, James D. G., 2006, *The Theology of Paul the Apostle*, Cambridge: Eerdmans.
Evans, Joseph, 'The Black Folks' Blues and Jazz Hermeneutic', *Journal of Religious Thought*, 60 (2008), pp. 125–48.
Fiddes, P., 'Ecclesiology and ethnography: Two disciplines, two worlds?' in Ward, P. (ed.), *Perspectives on Ecclesiology and Ethnography*, Grand Rapids, MI: Eerdmans. pp. 13–25.
Francis, Keith A., 2012, *The Oxford Handbook of the British Sermon 1689–1901*, Oxford Handbooks, Oxford: Oxford University Press.
Freeman, Lindsay Hardin, 2014, *Bible Women: All their Words and Why they Matter*, Kindle Edition, Forward Movement.
Gay, Doug, 2018, *God be in My Mouth: 40 Ways to Grow as a Preacher*, Edinburgh: St Andrew Press.
Graham, Elaine, 2017, *Apologetics without Apology: Speaking of God in a World Troubled by Religion*, Didsbury Lecture Series Book, Eugene, OR: Cascade.
Guilding, A., 1960, *The Fourth Gospel and Jewish Worship*, Oxford: Clarendon.
Gunning, Tom, 1994, *D. W. Griffith and the Origins of American Narrative Film: The Early Years at Biograph*, Urbana, IL: University of Illinois Press.
Heywood, David, 2013, *Transforming Preaching*, London, SPCK.
Hirst, Judy, 2006, *Struggling to be Holy*, London: Darton, Longman and Todd.
Horsley, R. A., 2002, *Jesus and Empire: The Kingdom of God and the New World*, Minneapolis: Fortress Press.
Hull, John M., 2011, *What Prevents Christian Adults from Learning?* London: SCM Press.
Hunsinger, George, 1993, *How to Read Karl Barth*, Oxford: Oxford University Press.
Jeanrond, Werner G., 1991, London: Palgrave Macmillan.
John of the Cross, 1959, *The Dark Night of the Soul*, trans. E. Allison Peers, New York: Doubleday.
Johnson, Keith L., 2010, *Karl Barth and the Analogia Entis*, Vol. 6, London: T&T Clark.
Johnson, Keith L., 2019, *The Essential Karl Barth: A Reader and Commentary*, Grand Rapids, MI: Baker.
Johnson, Patrick, 2015, *The Mission of Preaching: Equipping the Community for Faithful Witness*, Downers Grove, IL: InterVarsity Press.
Keller, Timothy, 2015, *Preaching: Communicating Faith in an Age of Scepticism*, London: Hodder and Stoughton.
Kimmel, M., 2016, *Privilege: A Reader*, New York: Routledge.

BIBLIOGRAPHY

Levine, Amy-Jill, 2015, *Short Stories by Jesus*, New York: HarperCollins.

Long, T. G., 2005, 'The Distance We Have Traveled: Changing Trends in Preaching' in Day, David, J. Astley and L. J. Francis, *A Reader on Preaching*, Aldershot: Ashgate, pp. 11–16.

Long, Thomas, 2005, *The Witness of Preaching*, 2nd edn, Louisville, KY: Westminster John Knox.

Long, Thomas, 2016, *The Witness of Preaching*, 3rd edn, Louisville, KY: Westminster John Knox.

Lowry, E., *The Homiletical Plot, expanded edition: the Sermon as Narrative Art Form*, Louisville, KY: Westminster John Knox Press.

Manning, L., D. Cassel & J. C. Cassel, 2013, 'St. Augustine's Reflections on Memory and Time and the Current Concept of Subjective Time in Mental Time Travel', *Behavioral Sciences (Basel, Switzerland)*, 3(2), pp. 232–43.

McKenzie, Alyce M., 2018, *Making a Scene in the Pulpit: Vivid Preaching for Visual Listeners*, Louisville, KY: Westminster John Knox.

Miles, S., 2012, *Take this Bread: A Radical Conversion*, Norwich: Canterbury Press.

Miller-McLemore, Bonnie J. (ed.), 2012, *The Wiley-Blackwell Companion to Practical Theology*, Oxford: Wiley-Blackwell.

Monshau, M., 'The Influence of Pope Benedict XVI's Liturgical Initiatives on Preaching Beyond Postmodernity,' *Antiphon: A Journal for Liturgical Renewal* 22(2) (2018), pp. 186–98.

Morrison, Stephen D., 2017, *Karl Barth in Plain English*, Columbus, OH: Beloved.

Newbigin, L., 1995, *Proper Confidence: Faith, Doubt, and Certainty in Christian Discipleship*, London: SPCK.

O'Leary, D., 2006, *Imagination: The Forgotten Dimension*, The Furrow.

Oakley, Lisa, and Justin Humphreys, 2019, *Escaping the Maze of Spiritual Abuse*, London: SPCK.

Oakley, M., 2016, *The Splash of Words: Believing in Poetry*, Norwich: Canterbury Press.

Oakley, M., 2019, *By Way of the Heart: The Seasons of Faith*, Norwich: Canterbury Press.

Parsenios, George, 'Anamnesis and the Silent Narrator in Plato and John', *Religions* 8 (2017), pp. 1–11.

Placher, William C., 'Teaching Christian Theology.' *Teaching Theology & Religion* 1, no. 1 (1998), pp. 36–47.

Powell, Mark A., 2001, *Chasing the Eastern Star: Adventures in Biblical Reader-Response Criticism*, Louisville, KY: Westminster John Knox Press.

Powell, Mark A., 2007, *What Do They Hear? Bridging the Gap between Pulpit and Pew*, Nashville, TN: Abingdon Press.

Radford, S., 'The New Homiletic within Non-Christendom', *Journal of the Evangelical Homiletics Society* 5(2), (2005), pp. 4–18.

Rapp, Claudia, 'Storytelling as Spiritual Communication in Early Greek Hagiography: The Use of Diegesis', *Journal of Early Christian Studies* 6, 3 (1998), pp. 431–48.

Reid, A., 1958, *Growing Flying Happening*, The New Yorker.

Ricœur, Paul, 2008, *From Text to Action*. London: Continuum.

Robb, Nigel J., 1999, *The Preaching Triangle*, Edinburgh: The Ministry Department of the Church of Scotland.

Schussler Fiorenza, Elisabeth, 1983, *In Memory of Her: A Feminist Theological Reconstruction of Christian Origins*, New York: Crossroad.

Shahraz, Q., 2001, *The Holy Woman*, Arcadia Books, Islamabad: Alhambra.

Slemmons, Timothy M., 'Between text & sermon: Philippians 3.17—4.1', *Interpretation: A Journal of Bible and Theology* 64(1), (2010), pp. 78–80.

Smith, J., 'Covering Peter Sutcliffe's crimes, I saw that women weren't listened to – and they still aren't', *The Guardian*, 13 November 2020, https://www.theguardian.com/commentisfree/2020/nov/13/peter-sutcliffe-crimes-women-police-investigation-murders-misogny accessed 4.3.21.

Sommers, Kat, 2016, '15 TV Shows that Broke the Fourth Wall', Anglophenia, BBC America. https://www.bbcamerica.com/anglophenia/2016/03/15-tv-shows-that-broke-the-fourth-wall accessed 4.5.21.

Stevenson, Peter K., 2017, *SCM Studyguide to Preaching*, London: SCM Press.

Storkey, E., 2015, *Scars Across Humanity: Understanding and Overcoming Violence Against Women*, London: SPCK.

Sweet, L., 2014, *Giving Blood: A Fresh Paradigm for Preaching*, Grand Rapids: Zondervan.

Swinton, J., 2017. *Becoming Friends of Time: Disability, Timefullness, and Gentle Discipleship*, London: SCM Press.

Taylor, Barbara Brown, 2009, *An Altar in the World: Finding the Sacred Beneath our Feet*, Kindle Edition, Norwich: Canterbury Press.

Taylor, Barbara Brown, 2014, *Learning to Walk in the Dark*, Kindle Edition, Norwich: Canterbury Press.

Thiselton, Anthony, 1977, 'The New Hermeneutic', in Marshall, I. Howard (ed.), *New Testament Interpretation: Essays on Principles and Methods*, pp. 308–33.

Thiselton, Anthony, 1992, *New Horizons in Hermeneutics*, Grand Rapids, MI: Zondervan.

Thiselton, Anthony, 2019, *2 Corinthians: A Short Exegetical and Pastoral Commentary*, Eugene, OR: Cascade.

BIBLIOGRAPHY

Vanhoozer, Kevin J., 1998, *Is there a Meaning in this Text?* Leicester: Apollos, IVP.

Vanhoozer, Kevin J., 2006, 'A Person of the Book? Barth on Biblical Authority and Interpretation' in Sung Wook Chung (ed.), *Karl Barth and Evangelical Theology*, Milton Keynes: Paternoster, pp. 26–59.

Viazovski, Yaroslav, 2015, *Image and Hope: John Calvin and Karl Barth on Body, Soul, and Life Everlasting*, Princeton Theological Monograph Series Book 221, Kindle Edition, Eugene, OR: Pickwick.

Wallace, M. I., 1995, *The Second Naiveté*, Macon, Georgia: Mercer University Press.

Werner Amram, D., 'Adultery' from the Jewish Encyclopedia, https://jewishencyclopedia.com/articles/865-adultery, accessed 4.3.21.

Wingren, G., 2004, *Luther on Vocation*, Eugene, OR: Wipf and Stock.

Wink, Walter, 1973, *The Bible in Human Transformation*, Minneapolis: Fortress.

Woods, Faye, 'Too Close for Comfort: Direct Address and the Affective Pull of the Confessional Comic Woman in *Chewing Gum* and *Fleabag*', *Communication, Culture & Critique* 12 (2019), pp. 194–212.

Wright, N. T., 2005, *Scripture and the Authority of God*, London: SPCK.

Wright, Tom, 2010, *Virtue Reborn*, London: SPCK.

Index of Bible References

OLD TESTAMENT

Genesis
1.31	160
18	55
28.16	34
32.24	87

Exodus
2.1–3	93
3.3	47
3.4	47
3.6	47–8
3.10	47–8
3.12	47–8

Leviticus
20.10	xv

Deuteronomy
26.5–7	134–5

Judges
19	166
21.25	9

Ruth
1.16	135

1 Samuel
3	55

2 Samuel
12.16–30	80

1 Kings
19.7–17	55

Job
38.12	160
38.16	160
39.26–27	160

Psalms
9.1	38
23	156
24	158–61
31.15	34
42	66
51.10	38
56.3	156
73.26	38, 40
139	73, 78
139.14	75

Proverbs
2.21	40–1
3.5	39
4.23	39
28.10	41

Isaiah
25.6–9	125
45.3	43
52.7–10	101–3
53	166–71

Jeremiah
18.1–6	50

Lamentations
3	43

NEW TESTAMENT

Matthew
2.1–2	90–1
2.3	91
2.7	91
3.15	137
3.17	137
4.1–11	136–41
5.3	140
5.6	140
5.10	140
6.33	140
13.3	140
13.31	140
13.44	140
15.19	39
19.14	140
19.17	49
20.1–16	35–6
28.20	156

Mark
1.4–11	148–53
1.35–39	57
7.1–8	96–7, 122

Luke
2.22–38	145–8
1.46–55	79
4.16–30	80

4.22	80	Acts		Ephesians	
8.40–56	55	16.16–40	107–8	2.1–10	161–6
12.13–34	153–7	16.17	107	4.14	130 (with 142 n14)
12.34	39	16.18	107		
13.31–35	104–7			6.18	37
15.1–10	122–3	Romans			
20.23	130 (with 142 n14)	8.14–39	166–71	Philippians	
				1.18	67 with n7
24.44–53	107–8	1 Corinthians			
		2.2	70	3.17—4.1	104–7
John		11.27–32	78		
1.1–14	101–3	13	41–2	Colossians	
1.38	92			3.2	39
2	48	2 Corinthians			
3.30	74	1.12	6	1 Timothy	
4.29	120	2.17	6, 69	1.12–17	122
8.3–11	xiv	4.2	130		
10.14–15	78	4.5–7	4–5	Hebrews	
11.20–44	125–9	4.7	xiii	1.1–4	101–3
11.21–27	127	4.13	25	4.14–16	166–71
11.27	36–7	5.16–17	5		
11.32	127	5.20	7	James	
11.35	36	11.3	130 (with 142 n14)	2.14–18	61
14	166–71				
15.4–7	53	11.11	3	1 Peter	
20.31	133	11.30	3	1.5–7	44
				2.23–25	44–5

Index of Names and Subjects

abiding in God 52–4
Abraham and Sarah 55
adultery xiv
Allen, Matt xv–xviii
  on Jesus' temptations 136–41
Alter, Robert 73
Ambrose (saint) 51
apologetics 24
Arthur (king) 125
Augustine 67
authority, shifted from preachers 19–20

Bailey, Kenneth 83
Bakhtin, Mikhail 94
Barth, Karl 7–10, 12, 14, 23
beachcombing 46–9
Bellini 146–7
bereavement 80
Bible
  as an Eastern book 83
  God speaking through 109
  interpretation 12, 49, 72, 110
  marginal notes 108–9
  as narrative 94
Brecht, Bertolt 131
Bretherton, Roger 92
Bridgman, Jenny, Candlemas sermon 145–8
Briggs, Melody 96, 121
Brown, Brené 41–2, 77–8
Brown, Tom 142 n17
Bruce, Kate 30, 50, 142 n13
  sermon on lockdown 161–6

Brueggemann, Walter 158, 161
Bultmann, Rudolph 72
Buttrick, David 17–18, 26 n3

Calvin, John 64–5
Cameron, Helen 31 n125
Campolo, Tony 50
Cana wedding 48
Carter, Sydney 89–90
clay jars 4–5, 7, 74–5, 130
climate emergency 159
communion service 134–5
Cooling, Margaret 93
copywriting 61–2
Craddock, Fred 13–17
Cranmer, Thomas 56
creativity 52
cultural heritage 82–3
curiosity 92–4

darkness 43–4, 89
death 163–4
deductive preaching 10–12
desire 66
despair 165
developmental sermons 11
direct address 131–2
dolly peg exercise 96–8, 121–2

Elijah 55
empathy 121–4
Eucharist 23
exegesis 72

Fleabag 131–3
Forster, E. M. 72
fourth wall 131–2

globalized society 81–5
God
  encounter with 64, 68, 114
  as King 45
  self-revelation 70
  wrestling with 87–8
Good Samaritan 98, 121
grace 9
Greer, Broderick 109
Gross, Nancy Lammers 22

heaven 106
Herod 90–1, 104
Hirst, Judy 65–6
holiness 65–6
Holy Spirit 150–2
homiletics 1–3
hope 120, 155–7
hospitality 78–9
Hull, John 52

imagination 10, 16, 50–1
Indian culture 83–4
inductive preaching 15–16

Jacob 87–8
Jairus 55
Jeremiah, and the potter's house 50
Jesus
  baptism 148–53
  as Lord 45
  reinterprets scripture 49
  reveals God's truth 61
  and time 36–7
  as vine 53
  wilderness temptations 136–41
  as Word of God 7
Jesus Prayer 56
John the Baptist 148–50
John of the Cross 89

journeying 88–90
journeys 52

Kimmel, Michael 74
Kingdom of God 106–7
Knowles, Andrew 70

lament 166–71
language 17
  in preaching 51–2, 116
Latz, Deirdre Brower, sermon on lament 166–71
Lazarus 99–100, 126, 138–9
Lectio Divina 56–7
life stage 81
light 89
location 79–80
lockdown 161–2
Long, Thomas 20–1, 52
losing and finding 122–4
love, Paul's definition of 41–2
Love, Joel 101–3
Lowry, E. 18–19
Luther, Martin, on vocations 54

McKenzie, Alyce 22
Magi 90–2
marriage 79–80
Martha 126–7
Mary and Martha 126–8
Mary (mother of Jesus) 146–8
masks 75–7
metaphoric language 16
Miles, Sarah 134
mindfulness 39, 56
Missio Dei 70
Moore, Simon, harvest sermon 153–7
Moses 47, 93
Muggles 162
Murphy, Steve 122–3
Muthalaly, Saju 60–1, 81–5

Naidu, Sarojini 84
narrative 94, 121
  sermons 15, 18–19

INDEX OF NAMES AND SUBJECTS

natural theology 9
New Homiletic 2–3, 13–22
Now Homiletic 3, 23–5, 134–5

Oakley, Mark 52, 116
O'Leary, Donal 50–1
openness 78–9

Paul (saint) 3–7
definition of love 41–2
pebbles making ripples 118–19
Pharisees 96–7, 104
pilgrims 52
place 79–80
playing 49–52
poetry 116
possessions 162
potter's house 50
Powell, Mark Allan 121
prayer
  canonical times 35
  stilling 56
preachers
  as ambassadors for Christ 7
  authority 19–20
  as clay jars 4–5, 7, 74–5
  as glass jars 10
  hope 120
  integrity 130
  personal faith of 23, 61, 132–3
  present 23–5, 33–57
  role 21
  as witnesses 21–2
  as wordsmiths 51–2
preaching
  aims 62–3, 67
  deductive 10–12
  encounter with God 64, 68
  liturgical context 63–4
  method 17
  relevance 113–14, 118
  shallow 120
  triangle 14
  as a way of life xii
  preconceived ideas 80, 110

prejudice, against women xii–xv, 71–2
progression 159
Puritans 11

Randolph, David 13
reason vs imagination 10, 11
repentance 105–6
revelation
  of God in Jesus 7–8, 61–2
  in God's activity 70
  in sermons 10
Ricœur, Paul 12

Samuel, hears God calling 55
Sarah, and Abraham 55
Schüssler Fiorenza, Elisabeth xv
seasons, of the church's year 42–6
seeking 92–3
sermons
  for All Saints 125–9
  for Ascension Day 107
  for Candlemas 145–8
  common core 69–70
  on creation 158–61
  as event of revelation 10
  examples 100–7, 145–71
  for Harvest 153–7
  on lament 166–71
  for Lent 104–7
  on lockdown 161–6
  for midnight mass 101–3
  preparation 65–8, 73, 78, 83, 119
  as shared journeying 52
  styles 10–12
Shahraz, Qaisra 115
Shercliff, Liz xii–xv
  sermon for Lent 104–7
shoes, taking them off 84
Simeon 146–8
sincerity 6
slave trade 71
still-heartedness 39–40

187

stories 115, 121, 123
Sweet, Leonard 115

Tagore, Rabindranath 84
talents 76
Taylor, Barbara Brown 44, 47, 54, 89
Thomas, Dylan 52
Thomas, Grace, sermon on creation 158–61
time 34–8
travelling 88–90

university sermons 10

Vashti 116–17
vocations 54

Watson, Tim 98–100
'we' 135–6

wealth 154, 162
wholeheartedness 39–42
Wink, Walter 28 n50
women
  prejudice against xii–xv, 71–2
  silenced 145–8
word clouds 69
Word of God 13–14, 110
  Jesus as 7
words
  as tool of preachers 51–2
  and understanding 13
worry 155
wrestling
  with Bible text 109
  with God 87–8
Wright, N. T. 94–5
Wyld, Rich, sermon on Jesus' baptism 148–53